Prai
Five Little Questi
Life God Designed for You

"For the woman who wants to reach her potential for God and good in the world, Dannah Gresh points the way by helping you answer five little questions. I highly recommend this book."

—Gary D. Chapman, Ph.D.
Author, *The Five Love Languages* and *The Five Languages of Apology*

"Dannah Gresh is one of the most insightful authors writing today. She knows her audience and is willing to be authentic concerning her own life struggles, which makes her not only credible but also worth reading. Every time she has been a guest on *Midday Connection*, we have received a significant number of e-mails attesting to her wisdom as a woman of God. If you really want to make a difference with your life, the kind that Dannah makes, pick up a copy of *Five Little Questions* and uncover the life God designed for you."

—Anita Lustrea
Host, *Midday Connection*

"I started out reading Dannah's book for an endorsement and ended up reading it for me. What a life-changing concept. Instead of pursuing purpose for its own sake, we should be pursuing freedom and flexibility; only then are we able to be moved into God's best purpose for our lives. For those of us who think being merely *busy* sounds like a rest cure, this is quite a knock over the head. But a very, very good one."

—Shaunti Feldhahn
Author, *For Women Only* and *For Young Women Only*

"Women today are running themselves ragged in the pursuit to find meaning and purpose in life. Dannah's book, *Five Little Questions That Reveal the Life God Designed for You*, provides women with a means to stop, take a deep breath, and do a simple self-inventory to ensure that they are building their lives on a firm foundation. Dannah has penned a prescription for what ails women today!"

—Vicki Courtney
Speaker and best-selling author, *Your Girl* and *TeenVirtue*

"Sometimes it's not a matter of having all the right answers but knowing what questions to ask. Dannah helps you identify the questions that only you and God can answer together to unlock the key to your life of freedom and purpose."

—Lisa Ryan
Speaker; cohost and reporter, *InTouch Ministries* and *700 Club*; and author, *For Such a Time as This*

FIVE
LITTLE
QUESTIONS

That REVEAL the LIFE GOD DESIGNED for YOU

DANNAH GRESH

FIVE
LITTLE
QUESTIONS

That REVEAL the LIFE GOD DESIGNED for YOU

THOMAS NELSON
Since 1798

NASHVILLE   DALLAS   MEXICO CITY   RIO DE JANEIRO   BEIJING

Published in Nashville, Tennessee. Thomas Nelson is a trademark of Thomas Nelson, Inc.

Thomas Nelson, Inc. titles may be purchased in bulk for educational, business, fund-raising, or sales promotional use. For information, please e-mail SpecialMarkets@ThomasNelson.com.

Library of Congress Cataloging-in-Publication Data

Gresh, Dannah.
    Five little questions that reveal the life God designed for you /
Dannah Gresh.
        p. cm.
    ISBN-10 0-7852-1244-2
    ISBN-13 978-0-7852-1244-7
    1. Christian women—Religious life. I. Title.
BV4527.G745 2006
248.8'43—dc22

                                        2006035728

Printed in the United States of America

07 08 09 10 11 RRD 5 4 3 2 1

To you, the woman
who will fight to
transcend her packed
schedule to find the
life God designed, full
of meaning and purpose.

Contents

My appointment for base color and highlights was cancelled today. The Northeast got hit with a blizzard, and the stylist couldn't get in to the salon.

Normally, I'm not one to care if my roots betray the illusion that I'm a blonde. However, I fly out for a major television interview in twenty-four hours to promote one of my books. The show claims an audience of 24 million viewers. Can you understand why I'd prefer to be completely blonde on this particular week?

It's OK. They got me rescheduled for tomorrow morning. (Thank you for breathing a sigh of relief along with me.)

It really works better for me to have this morning free. Well, it's far from free. I just swapped things around. I had to get copy to my designer for the PowerPoint slides I need for this weekend's speaking engagement in Atlanta. And my daughter, Lexi, seems to have racked up a triple-digit fine at the local library, so I have to make a quick stop there. I'm not the slightest bit angry with her. After all, she's working on her first research paper, and she's doing great! Since I'm in the middle of this big writing project, I can certainly understand what it's like to lose a few books in massive piles. Which reminds me, another reason I needed the extra time this morning is to please my editor by meeting my upcoming deadline. (How could I forget since I'm sitting here with my Starbuck's Chai, typing away?)

And I need to buy peanut butter today. Lots of it. Peanut butter, jelly, plastic knives. In seventeen days I'm leading a group of teenagers and chaperones on a mission trip to fight HIV/AIDS in

Africa. I've been there before. There's one stretch of land between two cities where I wouldn't let my dog eat the food.

So I need to pack peanut butter.

Why on earth am I telling you all this? Well, you may be having a similar day or have had one like it recently. Chaos! I don't mind it anymore. The chaos has culminated into a wondrous adventure ever since I've overcome my fears, enabling me to dive into the unbelievable adventure of living out the life God designed for me.

How on earth do we overcome the practical everyday limitations of budgets, responsibilities, and overwhelming fears to step into our own personal adventure of purpose?

Perhaps you've noticed that there's been a lot of talk about purpose lately. I love it. But often the books, experts, and sermons leave out one very important thing. How on earth do we overcome the practical everyday limitations of budgets, responsibilities, and overwhelming fears to step into our own personal adventure of purpose? How well my heart once knew the hopelessness of chaos without purpose. There were so many obstacles standing in the way to this adventure I now live in.

I think I should start at the beginning. You've got to see how bad it was. So let's go back a few years.

Oh, before we do, I'm just wondering: Do you think I should go with crunchy or creamy?

1

Are You Free to Live the Life God Designed for You?

Twelve years ago, I sat in my doctor's office, dreading the moments to come. How would I explain the drastic dichotomy between the woman she'd seen last night and the real me I'd reveal to her today? I decided not to stay, to blame it on not having enough time to wait . . . but the familiar rattle of the clipboard being removed from the door told me it was too late!

"Hello, Dannah," she greeted me. "What a bash last night!"

We made small talk about the grand gala my husband and I had hosted just hours ago. We'd had two hundred dozen white roses flown in from the Rose Bowl parade's growing fields. The hit of the party was the white chocolate dessert boxes with our magazine's logo imprinted in colored sugar. In my sequined gown and with my hair swept into a French twist, I'd presented one of my doctor's brave and pioneering cancer patients with our magazine's Woman of the Year Award. It was quite a bash.

Eventually we turned to the reason for my appointment. The glitz and glamour façade gave way to the dark cloud of emptiness that pervaded my life.

Tears flowed. "Well . . . I . . . ahhh." I stalled. "I'm so tired all the time. But it's more than that. It's like there's this thick cloud covering me. I feel so . . ."

1

My mind raced for words. I couldn't speak. What was wrong with me? Wasn't I the woman who'd recently led the first community effort to raise thousands of dollars to fight child abuse? Wasn't I a member of the by-invitation-only Junior Club who'd partied our way through a year of craft sales, "duck derbies," and parlor tours? Wasn't it my husband and I who'd brought life to our little advertising market with a magazine and our two radio stations? Wasn't I the one who'd pulled off vacation Bible school when the director quit? Yes I was.

And the dark cloud was there at every event.

Even at home with my "million-dollar family"—one boy and one baby girl—I felt disconnected and confused. I woke up most days wishing I could sleep them out.

"I feel . . ." I attempted to speak but still couldn't find the words.

Through my uncontrollable crying I heard pieces of my doctor's kind counsel:

". . . depression . . . lack of serotonin in the brain . . . antidepressants . . ."

She handed me a prescription.

"Dannah," she encouraged, "you really need to slow down. Find what really matters and do just that."

Doesn't it all matter? *I asked myself on the way home.* Isn't that why I do it?

I realized then that I didn't know.

———

Are you free to pursue the life God designed for you? Maybe it's a little easier to digest if I simply ask, "Are you free?"

I don't mean to be so personal so fast, but . . .

Are you free?

When the alarm clock goes off, do you dread the day? Or do you feel free to rise from bed with passion for what's ahead?

Are you in bondage to a paycheck . . . or maybe two? Or are you free to do what you absolutely love with your life?

Do you fear your credit card will be declined because you are shackled to debt? Or are you free from such heaviness, knowing that your bank account is healthy—not necessarily filled to the brim but wisely preserved so that you have confidence in your spending?

Does fear continually lock you in its prison of consuming thoughts over unachieved life dreams such as being married? becoming a mother? running a marathon? getting a promotion? Or are you free to enjoy life just as it is until such wondrous gifts come along?

Are you enslaved to the status and titles of a career? Or could you freely walk away from them if being all you were meant to be required such courage?

Are you afraid you might run into this person or that one because you're enslaved to broken relationships? jobs gone bad? broken business deals? Or are you free to enjoy long-lasting and faithful friendships?

Do you have a sense of guilt over the relationships that *are* broken (everyone has some) and a lack of resolution? Or are you free to approach God with the wounded places from them?

Are you free?

Transcending Your Packed Schedule

I think the answer for far too many of us is no. The world's paradigm of success has slaughtered our passion and the very core

The five little questions reveal
God's best life for you.

of our purpose. We're like rats on spin-
ning wheels, wondering where we're going
and getting nowhere. We're not free. And we
fear we never will be.

Do you see it? Do you feel it?

I see it. I *have* felt it. And I'm not alone.

Half of all women in the United States would like
to "transcend their packed schedules to figure out the
meaning and purpose of their life."[1] Are you one of
them? Make yourself a cup of tea and curl up with me.
I can show you how to transcend your packed schedule
to find the freedom to pursue your life's meaning and
purpose.

You see, I was once in bondage. By the very naive
age of twenty-two, my husband and I had started both
a family and a marketing agency that served several
Midwestern state banks, service agencies, and multi-
million-dollar retail chains. The market wasn't well
served, so we easily became the regional experts in marketing. By the age of twenty-five we'd added a magazine
and two radio stations and were operating a three-
pronged company with more than twenty employees.
We were collecting marketing awards from the likes of
Inc. Magazine, and the state government had recognized our leadership in economic development market-

ing. Yes, I was driven. And, at the same time, I was hopelessly enslaved to a schedule that strangled the life out of my passions.

I was not free.

I felt it to the core of my being.

Underneath the awards, community positions, cash flow, and church service, I was tired, weepy, sad, confused, and sometimes even angry. Rick Warren says, "People who don't know their purpose try to do too much—and it causes stress, fatigue and conflict."[2] I have known that place of existence. How very enslaved I felt to the pace of it all. The problem for me wasn't that I didn't believe my life had a bigger, better purpose than the chaos I was living in. I just didn't know the practical steps I needed to take to get out of the obligations of my life to pursue the call on my life. It made me angry, tired, and stressed. I felt I might always be one who dreamed of my purpose rather than one who actually lived it out.

Half of all women in the United States would like to "transcend their packed schedules to figure out the meaning and purpose of their life."[1] I can show you how.

Seeking Freedom

A lot has been written on purpose since Rick Warren's record-breaking bestseller *The Purpose Driven Life* was released. I'm not trying to write a book on purpose. Warren's book, the flurry of related books that followed, and even some that came before, like Henry Blackaby's *Experiencing God: Knowing & Doing the Will of God*, have certainly done the subject justice.

What hasn't been explained is just how on earth we rise up

out of the enslavement of our current situation to reach out for that purpose. How do we find time to pursue God's best when we're locked into a life of routine, debt, and obligations?

I found the purpose of my life, not in pursuing it but in seeking freedom from my fears and overwhelming responsibilities. When I was burdened with the routine life of too many responsibilities and not enough zeros in my paychecks, I'd have never believed that God could actually *expand* my responsibility to include a national ministry for teens and women plus a ministry to fight HIV/AIDS in Zambia, Africa. I didn't set out to find these things, which every day give me joy and purpose and pleasure. I set out to get free. After I found freedom, God released me—not to less, but to more! The irony of it is this: People *think* I'm working so hard. They sometimes ask me how I "do it all." The secret is that I've never worked less and achieved so very much. It all came quite unexpectedly when I began to pursue freedom.

We're going to dig into the Bible for truth about freedom. We're going to look at common fears that each of us face as women and that drain us of our passion to live out the life God specifically designed for us. Then, fears laid down, we'll determine if any of the discouragement in your life is God's nudge for you to make some changes because you've designed your own life. (Very dangerous territory. Trust me.) Or if you are living in the purpose of your life but just can't feel it. Finally, we'll get practical. I've got five questions for you to answer in relation to your life. I truly believe that if you slow down and answer these five questions thoroughly, you'll have an action plan to live out the fulfilling and adventuresome life that God designed for you. I just can't wait to see these questions become useful in your life. As you answer each one, you'll uncover gifts you've missed, talents you'd forgotten, dreams that need pursuing, and perhaps even pursuits that need to be dropped.

> If you slow down and answer these five questions thoroughly, you'll have an action plan to live out the fulfilling and adventuresome life that God designed for you.

Best of all, we're going to stand in awe of God and wonder at the secrets we discover about other great men and women of faith. You won't believe the stuff I've dug up about great people of the faith such as C. S. Lewis and David Livingstone. We'll go all the way back to Peter and David. Why, I've even got some scoop to dish out on contemporary leaders—author Brennan Manning and spokeswoman for international adoption Mary Beth Chapman. We're even going to look at today's mainstream Christian models such as athlete Kurt Warner, Secretary of State Condoleeza Rice, political advisor Karen Hughes, and New York Times best-selling author Donna VanLiere. Their rise from the rat race into the race for greatness inspires me! I think it'll inspire you to join them.

Hold it. Do you fear you cannot possibly put your name on this list? Does it just seem as though you don't belong? Oh my! Is that proof that you're living under the bondage of our first fear?

It's time to unleash some truth in your life!

Making It Work

I love books that change my life. The ones that change my life usually require me to roll up my sleeves and do a little work. At the end of each chapter, I'll be inviting you to do just that.

There are two ways to do this:

You can just simply grab a journal and write a letter to God after each chapter. Journaling enables you to live out what you read. If you select this option, you'll simply journal a letter to God based on a question I give you right here. Your question for this chapter is this: Are you free?

Your second option lets you go much deeper. You can purchase the *Five Little Questions That Reveal the Life God Designed for You* study guide. It's like having me as a personal life coach during your journaling activity. The study guide is your journal, but it's filled with specific questions, quizzes that help you answer them, diagrams, and Scriptures to treasure. In it you have the tools to create a "M.A.P." (My Action Plan) to the life God designed for you.

Visit my Web site to learn more about it:

www.purefreedom.org

PART ONE

FIVE FEARS THAT STAKE US TO MEDIOCRE LIVES

"Courage is resistance to fear, mastery of fear—not absence of fear."

—Mark Twain

Fear #1: There's No Hope for Me

Here I was. Running. Again.

I'd planned an expensive week at the beach with my family to get away from it all. Perhaps if I got Bob away from his work and me from mine, we'd find some remnant of passion for each other . . . some connection to each other besides the bills. Maybe this rest would give me what I needed to overcome the depression or at least offer a glimmer of hope that I could overcome it.

This was not how our getaway was supposed to look. The reservations I'd made had fallen through. We saw "no vacancy" signs everywhere. The kids and I were stranded at the beach while Bob went angrily looking for someplace to stay.

"Enjoy it," he said coldly when he dropped us off at the beach. "I imagine we'll be driving back today."

I sat with my feet in the waves, crying. I pleaded with God to change things, to help us, and to rescue us from everything . . . from this small disappointment to the constant financial fears that pushed us to work endless hours. My prayer was desperate and selfish.

Through the veil of tears, something in the sand caught my eye. Each time the white foam of ocean waves caressed my feet, it was leaving me a treasure. There were dozens if not hundreds of them— the tiniest little white clams I'd ever seen. Each one was no bigger than a pea. The crashing waves left them on top of the sand in the bright sun, which could no doubt relentlessly scorch them in no time at all. Instead, within seconds, they all suddenly stood on end in unison, stopping briefly like little soldiers at attention. And then, the dance began. They'd wriggle and jiggle their way back into the dark, cool depths of the moist sand, leaving only little air bubbles as proof that they had been there for a few brief moments.

I watched mesmerized as again and again they danced for me. In a moment of eureka, I realized that their dance was God's gift of protection.

I began to cry again. But this time I cried great, overwhelming tears of happiness as unspeakable joy swept over every part of my being. I reached my hands to heaven with delight, and I spontaneously erupted into praising God for these little clams. I could not help myself. It didn't matter to me if anyone saw.

Perhaps I'd found what I was looking for on this trip after all. There it was. The remnant. The glimmering coal of hope.

If God could take care of these little clams, He could take care of me.

———————

Hope is born of suffering.

Our spirits rise up to grasp hope when the doctor says, "It's cancer."

We have little but hope to reach for when the World Trade Centers fall.

We even eventually find our way to hope's door after Enron takes our life's savings.

It seems in the face of the worst of suffering, hope comes quickly. But where is the friendship between hope and suffering when that which causes the suffering is mundane, normal, common? When it's *just how it is?* Where is the hope when we can't find the courage to get out of bed to work two jobs for even one more day? to try one more time to pass that difficult class? to run at a breakneck pace for one more week? to juggle the demands of family and career? or to reach out for a dream our friends and family don't believe in? Where is the hope when our spirits tell us our lives are drastically off course? Where is hope in *this* suffering?

They say baby circus elephants are trained for self-bondage. Trainers wrap heavy chains around the elephants' chubby young legs and attach them to immovable steel stakes. As they grow, they never realize they could now walk off with little effort. By the time they weigh five or six tons, a simple little rope and a wooden stake will enslave them to the back of the circus tent for a lifetime of quiet labor.

I shudder just to think that you or I could be staked to a mediocre lifetime of quiet labor void of adventure and purpose. So many are shackled to the fear that "there's no hope for me." Oh, they can believe some people are meant to live exciting, fulfilling, purpose-filled lives, just not them. I once was one of these.

Are you one of them?

Do you think this is *just how it is?*

Many are shackled to the fear that "there's no hope for me." Oh, they can believe some people are meant to live exciting, fulfilling, purpose-filled lives, just not them.

Tell that to Condoleeza Rice. She was born in Birmingham, Alabama, at a time when racism was the catalyst for hideous hatred suffered by African Americans. She was eight years old when she felt her church floor shake under her feet. Two blocks away, the Ku Klux Klan had exploded a bomb in another African-

American church and killed four precious little girls . . . one of them Condoleeza's classmate.

At the time, the first words little African-American children were taught to read were "COLOREDS ONLY" so they would use the correct restroom or water fountain.

I guess no one told Condoleeza that there were signs plastered all over American leadership reading *white males only*. Or maybe she just chose to ignore them. Perhaps she, unlike the rest of us, knew no fear. Probably not. I'm sure she knew the very real fear that there just might not be any hope for her, but her parents never let it settle into her.

> The Bible warns that you will not find the hope for freedom in conventional wisdom, but that the great, exciting, blessed riches of God's purpose for your life are "hidden" (Eph. 3:8–9).

"My parents," says Condoleeza, "had me absolutely convinced that, well, you may not be able to have a hamburger at Woolworth's, but you can be president of the United States."[1]

She's the first African-American woman to become Secretary of State. She sits in one of the highest offices on the globe. She's been called *the most powerful woman in the world*. She didn't just accept "how it was." Regardless of what you think of her politics, a woman simply has to respect the tenacious fight for hope that is obviously under her peaceful façade.

Before the world was created, God's Spirit breathed purpose into the life of Condoleeza Rice. It was not to accept things as "just how it is," but to be a living, breathing example of African-American excellence in one of the highest offices in the United States of America.

This is what she was called to hope for. It is her freedom from the racial oppression she knew as a little girl. It is her purpose in life to stomp that oppression out with credible, intelligent leadership.

The Hope for Freedom

Hope looks different for each of us. And that's where it gets challenging. The Bible warns that you will not find the hope for freedom in conventional wisdom, but that the great, exciting, blessed riches of God's purpose for your life are "hidden" (Eph. 3:8–9). That doesn't mean you *can't* find your purpose. The Greek word *anexichnias-ton*—don't ask me to say that—is what ends up in our Bibles as "hidden." It meant "that which cannot be traced by human footprints." So enter the rat race if you want, but I think you'll find that those human footprints won't lead you to the great, exciting, blessed riches of God's freedom for you. To find those, you have to follow the sovereign footprints of God.

Ephesians 1:18 reads, "I pray also that the eyes of your heart may be enlightened in order that you may know the hope to which he has called

How on Earth Will We Ever See the Footprints of God?

Incidentally, they have been followed. Evidence of this is found in a reference to the Israelites as they journeyed from Egypt, their place of bondage, to freedom. Psalm 77:19 says, "Your path led through the sea, your way through the mighty waters, though your footprints were not seen." They didn't see them, but they followed them. And so must we, but how? How do we follow them if we cannot see them? That's one of our greatest challenges.

15

you, the riches of his glorious inheritance." Since we're tracing something that human eyes cannot see, we've got to look with the eyes of our hearts. Eyes that only God can supernaturally open.

Unfortunately, we live with such a powerful paradigm of the physical world that we can have a hard time shifting from our physical eyes to our spiritual hearts. We need God to open the eyes of our hearts.

The Eyes of Our Hearts

Donna VanLiere, author of the *New York Times* bestseller *The Christmas Shoes* and its sequels, *The Christmas Blessing* and *The Christmas Hope*—each one gets better—has been a dear friend of mine since college. She is well acquainted with the suffering that begets hope. She writes:

> When I was a child, a local television station would play all the great old movies and musicals on weekends. I'd watch them and was mesmerized. I wanted to grow up and marry a man like those leading men and have three or four children. That was my dream.

But God had a bigger dream—a greater purpose—for Donna's desire to be a mother. To live in it, her childhood dream had to die. She walked into the great suffering that infertility creates. I cried with her, prayed for her, and believed with her, but my hopes couldn't reach the lonely place in her heart. And her hopes were not being realized. After a few years, Donna began to make the great paradigm shift from praying for her physical body to praying for her spiritual heart:

"I would pray, 'Lord, fix my body. Fix Troy's body.' But the more I read the Scriptures, the more I realized that sometimes our dreams and plans have to die, so I started praying, 'Lord, fix my heart.'"

And as Donna's heart began to let go of one dream, a new one was literally birthed. Halfway around the world, God had His special angels guarding a bundle on the streets of the Guangxi Province in Southern China . . . a bundle that had been abandoned. A police officer noticed it and took that precious bundle to an orphanage. And in March of 2002, Grace Zhenli VanLiere was placed into the arms of her mother, Donna VanLiere.

> I wanted everything to go according to my dreams and plans, but God had a better way. I cannot imagine our life without Gracie in it. If I hadn't slowed down to seek God's plan, I would have missed one of the greatest blessings of my life.[2]
> —Donna VanLiere, author, *The Christmas Shoes* and *The Angels of Morgan Hill*

Donna learned to look with the eyes of her heart. Where did she look? She looked into the very center of her fear. At the core of her hopelessness. Her fear of never being a mother. Never holding a precious child she could call her own. She looked with spiritual eyes rather than with her physical eyes.

Having a hard time finding hope? It's time to look with the eyes of your heart, my friend. Only then can you see the hope God desires to pour into you so you can follow His footprints to His perfect plan.

The bottom line is that you cannot move forward in freedom hoping in dreams that God is not bringing to fruition. Are you prepared, like my friend Donna, to relinquish those unrealized dreams that God never planned to be yours? Even Condoleeza Rice had to let go of a very precious dream—to be a world-famous concert pianist—to follow the hope of her calling. Painful as it may seem, the place of our suffering is the place where we find the hope for freedom to live the life God designed for us. Embracing it gives us the courage to move past our fears.

Afraid there's just no hope for you? Look with the eyes of your heart. There is hope.

Making It Work

I pray also that the eyes of your heart may be enlightened in order that you may know the hope to which he has called you, the riches of his glorious inheritance.

—Ephesians 1:18

In what area of your life have you spent time, desperately looking with physical eyes, disabling your spiritual eyes to guide you into the life God designed for you? Talk to the Lord about that in a letter to Him.

3

Fear #2: Nothing Will Ever Satisfy Me

"Today, I'd like to try something a little different," explained Tippy. "Are you willing to give it a try?"

"Well, what is it?" I asked. Over the past six months, the medication had done its work. No longer armed with antidepressants but with some new rules about how much and when I could work, I was stabilized. No more teary outbursts or feelings of overwhelming anxiety. No more cloud of confusion or sleeplessness. I was feeling fully capable. I just wasn't satisfied. My life's work wasn't fulfilling to me. I knew that I had a long way to go. I was willing to try just about anything.

"I'm going to pray over you, and we're going to ask the Lord to give you a picture of what needs to be adjusted in your life," she said.

"Hmmmm? OK. I guess," I said, not believing for a moment that this was going to work.

Tippy began to pray and to affirm my ability to hear from God. She prayed for a long time and then was silent. We sat there in the silence. I expected nothing.

Then, as suddenly as if I were dreaming, a picture came into my head. It was crystal clear. I saw a glowing neon ring. It was huge. Deep in its center, I stood looking weak and worn. On my shoulders were dozens and dozens of people. My husband. My children. My coworkers. My church friends. My colleagues who sat on community boards with me. They all looked angry and frustrated, demanding and unsatisfied. There was no sound in my mind, but if there had been, it would have been a four-lane highway during rush hour—chaos!

The very core of my being ached. This was so very representative of my life. Nothing I worked for satisfied me, and it never seemed to satisfy those I was working to please.

I opened my eyes and told Tippy what I saw.

"What does it mean?" she asked.

"I don't know," I said with a hollow voice as I held back tears. "It doesn't mean anything."

"Yes, it does," said Tippy. "Do you think this is how you're meant to look—'weak' and 'worn'?"

I shrugged. Seemed it was just how it was. Life was destined to be hard and unsatisfying.

"Dannah," said Tippy, "I'm going to pray again, and I want you to ask God to show you if that is how your life is supposed to look."

I hadn't become more confident of this process, but I was eager to get rid of the pain in my heart. I closed my eyes. Tippy began to pray.

Immediately, I saw an entirely different picture. The ring was still there, glowing in its neon brilliance. But inside the circle was just me. I looked good. I looked great, really. And all those people, well, they were outside the ring. Bob and the children were so close that they were touching the ring. My friends from church were further away but still close. My coworkers were quite a way off. Everyone looked peaceful, content, satisfied.

I opened my eyes with a knowing look.

"Well," asked Tippy. "What did you see?"

"I saw my life as it should be," I said with certainty. "But how do I get there?"

In my bondage to this world—the schedules and clubs and tasks—I finally became thirsty. Desperately thirsty. I'd found that all the streams I was drinking from—success and titles and stuff—left me dissatisfied. Here I was, working hard to achieve all of my dreams, but I wasn't remotely satisfied. I began to fear I never could be.

About the time that I was being treated by my physician for chemical depletions, God led me to a wise Christian counselor who remains one of my most significant spiritual mentors—Tippy Duncan. I'd decided that I was thirsty enough to try anything and everything all at once. I'm glad I did. God used her to lead me to a place of true satisfaction. If all I'd done was treat the problem with antidepressants, it would have been like using crutches for a severely broken leg without ever setting it. It would never heal properly, and I'd be enslaved to a life of lameness, which would force me into dependency on the crutches forever.

I had many broken places in my life. The crutch of an antidepressant got me standing up so I could figure things out. Truly the pace of my life had created very real, very challenging physical results. The antidepressants allowed my brain to heal from overwork, but the real healing came from my time with God.

If all I'd done was treat the problem with antidepressants, it would have been like using crutches for a severely broken leg without ever setting it . . . I'd be enslaved to a life of lameness, which would force me into dependency on the crutches forever.

A few summers ago I spoke at a camp in the mountains of Northern California. Those mountains are an oxymoronic place in June. Ninety-degree days. A dry, warm, sun-filled heat. Patches of winter snow. Ice-covered lakes and ponds.

The sun was working hard to melt the winter remnants, sending the little creek just behind my cabin into a noisy fury. One morning I meditated on Psalm 42:1. It says, "As the deer pants for streams of water, so my soul pants for you, O God." I wondered if the deer ever became so thirsty that they'd venture into the very populated campsite to steal a drink of this icy water. Could it be that their thirst sometimes became great enough that they overcame their fear of man to dip into the rushing cool creek?

Suddenly, as if God were listening to just me . . .

Just then.

Just because.

There before me stood a sweet deer.

Five or six cabins boxed us in. The scent of man was everywhere. Her thirst was great.

I picked up my journal and wrote, "Oh, my God, let my thirst for You overflow within me, numbing me to my fears and complacency." Meditation on God's Word continues to be a powerful conduit to peace. My first experience with it—seeing the neon ring while meditating with Tippy—was a defining moment for me. Until that day, I wasn't quite sure I believed anything would ever satisfy me. That collision of God's truth and prayer that Tippy helped to create knocked me silly. Made me thirsty. I desperately wanted the peace that I saw when I closed my eyes the second time. The peace that the Bible promises. In one quick blink of an eye, God had assured me that His plan would satisfy.

This workaholic didn't waste any time digging right in. I have the drive to get things done, and so I dug into as many books as I could find to learn just how to find that place of holy satisfaction . . . a place where my passion for God would be spontaneous.

Christian Hedonism

John Piper, author of *Desiring God*, says that spontaneous passion for God is like the shipwrecked swimmer who gains sight of a shore and does not take the time to determine how he will try to reach it. He does not cognitively analyze to what extent he is pleased with this sighting. His desire explodes within him, and he responds.

It is like the seemingly tiny human who stands at the edge of the Grand Canyon for the first time. She does not ask herself, *To what end do I feel awe and wonder of this beauty?* She responds with sparkling eyes and smiles and invites those around her to enjoy the view with her. "Wow! Can you see that? Can you hear the river raging down there? Look. Look over there. Do you see the sun lighting the side of the canyon as if it were a masterful painting? Look over there . . ."[1]

Let me add that spontaneous passion for God is like a crazed woman sitting on the shore, watching tiny clams dance down into the sand. The woman does not cognitively say, "God cares for these clams, and He cares for me. I think that is good." No! She bursts into tears of joy and raises her

---

The Chief End of Man

My research led to a document called The Westminster Confession of Faith.

Biblical scholars appointed by Parliament began writing it as a thorough interpretation of how a Christian should live.

It is best known for its widely supported statement of the purpose of man. Perhaps you've heard these words. See if you can fill in the blanks.

"The chief end of man is to

_____

and

to_____."

---

hands and praises Him out loud in front of all the passersby.

Because John Piper has found such pleasure in God, he's come to call himself a Christian hedonist. I liked that. I wanted to be a Christian hedonist.

I just wasn't quite comfortable with what I might have to give up to find this life of being a Christian hedonist. Sleep. Power lunches. Another hour of adrenaline-rushing work. A position on a community board. Please understand. I was a Christian. I was convinced that God was the answer. I was involved at church. I was in a Bible study. But I was not remotely satisfied by God. I didn't enjoy Him. I wasn't drinking deeply.

My soul was thirsty.

We cannot find the satisfaction of God through His dreams for us if we are seeking the satisfaction this world says we deserve. There is sacrifice involved.

God was asking me to sacrifice in order to seek Him with all my heart and soul and mind. I'd need to go deeper for my wracking sense of duty to give way to satisfaction in God and in life. The odd part of this deep satisfaction is that it is effectively married to duty. (We'll explore this more deeply later on.) We cannot find the satisfaction of God through His dreams for us if we are seeking the satisfaction this world says we deserve. There is sacrifice involved.

I wasn't sacrificing to know God. I was just going along with the crowd and seeking satisfaction in paychecks, titles, and busyness. Before I was willing to make the sacrifice to follow hard after God, I had to first get to the point in my own life of being so desperate that there seemed to be no alternative but

God. I had to get thirsty like the little deer that faced her fears to come near my cabin's stream.

Are You Thirsty?

I'm thoroughly convinced that there is no other stream than that of a radical relationship with the living, loving God of the universe. I've had my fill of others, including a half-hearted sense of duty to God. *This* is the only one that satisfies.

Is it free of sacrifice? No. It's not. The first step in dipping into the satisfaction of God is letting go of our futile quests for satisfaction outside of Him. Our fear that we'll never really be satisfied is entirely true . . . if we're seeking satisfaction in our own dreams and hopes. However, if we relinquish those dreams and hopes and begin to look with the eyes of our hearts to sacrificially follow God's dreams, we can step into the fullest place of satisfaction.

> The first step in dipping into the satisfaction of God is letting go of our futile quests for satisfaction outside of Him. Our fear that we'll never really be satisfied is entirely true . . . if we're seeking satisfaction in our own dreams and hopes.

Isaiah 55:1–2 reads, "The Lord says, 'All you who are thirsty, come and drink . . . Why work for something that doesn't really satisfy you? Listen closely to me, and you will eat what is good; your soul will enjoy the rich food that satisfies'" (NCV).

What a sensible passage. Why work for something that doesn't really satisfy? Why work a job just for a paycheck to pay bills? (If your job doesn't have a deeper sense of purpose, it will never truly satisfy.) Why attend a parents association club only to

27

fill time? (But if you could share your worldview with someone who would never, ever set foot in a church, it could be ultimately fulfilling.) Why bake cookies for Bible school just because you were the next on the phone list? (If you love baking cookies, bake, bake, bake. If you don't love baking cookies, say no and ask God what He would like you to do with your time.) Why work for something that doesn't satisfy? The only way you'll find work satisfying is if it is directed by God's dream for your life.

Laying down your fear that nothing will ever satisfy might involve some painful sacrifice. This journey for freedom is wild and untamed. There are risks, but none of them greater than the risk of the living death you'll know if you don't drink of the full satisfaction of God's purpose for your life.

So are you working for things that don't satisfy? Are you thirsty?

Come! I promise, you'll be satisfied.

Making It Work

The Lord says, "All you who are thirsty, come and drink . . . Why work for something that doesn't really satisfy you? Listen closely to me, and you will eat what is good; your soul will enjoy the rich food that satisfies."

—Isaiah 55:1–2 NCV

Do you enjoy God? Oh, there is so much in that question. Ponder it deeply as you answer it in your journal with all the truthfulness you can muster!

4

Fear #3: There's No Time to Fix It

Tap, tap, tap.

"What on earth?" I grumbled, turning over to see that my alarm clock read 6:00 AM.

Tap, tap, tap. *Someone was at my back door. A rush of adrenaline surged through me at the oddity of it all.*

I wish Bob were here, I thought as I rolled out of bed and wrapped myself in a robe. I turned the short corner from my bedroom door to the country kitchen and glanced at the glass French doors that led to our deck.

Nothing.

I quickened my step to see whom I'd missed. I opened the door. No one.

Hmmmm? *I thought. Someone's funny idea of a prank.*

I headed back to bed. I nestled deeply down into the warm comforter. My bed had never felt so wonderful.

"Oh my!" I exclaimed, my eyes opening wide. I suddenly remembered the simple prayer I'd prayed last night as I drifted off to sleep. It had been another chaotic week, and I'd not paused one time to be with God. Not really. Nothing beyond a quick list of requests anyway.

More and more I was sensing God's call to spend time with Him. The vision that I'd received when Tippy prayed over me was becoming a deep desire in my heart. I was seeing that picture of the neon

31

ring surrounding only God and me. My heart was awakening to a need for a holy space for just the two of us. How I wanted it. I just wasn't sure how to get out of this place where everyone and every-thing else consumed my time. Certainly God understood my predica-ment. I'd set my alarm several times with ambitious plans to start the day alone with God, but I couldn't overcome the temptation to hit the snooze button. Again and again, I kept squeezing God out. I just didn't have time.

"God, I really want this. I just can't seem to work it in. If You'll awaken me, I'll meet You," I prayed.

Tap, tap, tap.

I jumped from my bed this time and ran to the doors. No one.

Tap, tap, tap.

This time I got down on my hands and knees, determined to catch whomever it was playing this prank.

Tap, tap, tap.

I stealthily crawled out and waited under the kitchen table. Feeling far more like a secret agent than a young mother, I tight-ened the belt on my fuzzy bathrobe.

Tap, tap, tap. Flutter!

A robin. It was a robin. Standing on the deck, she had to jump up to poke her little head above the wooden panel on the door frame. As she did, she'd flap her wings and peck the glass three times. I watched amazed.

"Could this be my wake-up call from God?" I marveled.

It would be the beginning of a rich and powerful quest to enter into that holy ring of space where I could commune with the God of the universe as if I . . . as if He . . . had nothing else to do but call us together.

Perhaps one of the greatest sacrifices God has required of me in order to live in freedom is the giving of my time to Him. When I began my quest for freedom, I was absolutely convinced that I did not have time for one more thing in my hectic schedule. It seemed I couldn't squeeze in more than ten minutes of time with God. And did I *really* need more than that? Yes, I did.

And, yes! For several mornings a robin did actually wake me with her gentle "tap, tap, tap." My son, though he was very young and does not remember it, saw the bird. I was so excited with the overwhelming possibility that the God of the universe was calling to me that I woke him and carried him to sit under the dining room table with me. As we waited, I explained, "God sent a bird to wake up Mommy to pray, Robby!"

Pretty soon it came.

Tap, tap, tap.

His eyes were wide as pancakes as he clapped his hands in delight. Together we applauded God's glory.

The bird never came back for an early-morning encounter, but I did. The rush I got from being with God—really, truly being with Him, not just passing by Him—was inexplicable. Instead of power lunches, I headed out to the local community park and had lunch with God every day. If that were impossible, I would hide away in a bubble bath after I put the kids to bed. But I was clearly staking my claim. I wanted to have time alone with my God.

For me, it seemed to take a full hour. Fifteen or twenty minutes didn't tear my heart away from the world. I was still consumed with client meetings, bills to be paid, the kids, the grocery list, and the house. My body still clamored to be at Kyoto for my favorite chicken teriyaki boxed lunch or at La Posada, munching on chips dipped in their famous homemade salsa. The appetites and pulls of the world were so strong for me. Still are, quite honestly.

My Routine with God

Psalm 63:1 became an anchor for me during days of overcoming the fear that I didn't have enough time: "God, you are my God. I search for you. I thirst for you like someone in a dry, empty land where there is no water" (NCV).

I learned that the word search *in the Hebrew meant "dawn, early rising, in immediate pursuit." If you're thirsty enough, you'll make God the first priority of your day. Truly, in the core of my being, I am not a morning person. But I never fail to start my day with a brief but meaningful prayer to God. I'm usually in the shower when I mutter something*

But after about thirty or forty minutes of just soaking in the presence of God as I read His Word, meditated, sang praise songs, and journaled my fears and hopes to Him, my physical desires felt less urgent, and I was able to tap into my spiritual passion to be with Him. It's still this way. I need focused time away from the world, and then—I really feel Him. His radiance begins to break through my brokenness and to cover me in peace.

Time with Him Multiplies the Time in Your Day

Convinced you don't have time? Proverbs 9:11 reads, "Through me your days will be many, and years will be added to your life." I see this in an hourly way on the days I'm with Him. I actually seem to have more hours in the day, and things are accomplished more easily. In fact, the New Living Translation uses the word *multiply* to refer to the reward of time that's turned back to us when we give our time to earnestly pursue God.

On the contrary, John 15:5 reads, "I am the vine; you are the branches. If a man remains in me and I in him, he will bear much fruit; apart from me you can do nothing." How many people are getting absolutely nothing done, all the while having terribly overloaded lives? You can spin and spin on the world's wheel of works and get nowhere, can't you?

Afraid there's no time to fix your life? No time to give solitude to God? Think again. Girl, you don't have the time *not* to start with God. If your list is as long as mine, do yourself a favor . . .

Be with Him first. *Do* the day later.

The fear that we don't have enough time isn't really a legitimate fear at all. It's an excuse. One that, if we look with the eyes of our flesh, seems really valid, but we aren't looking with physical eyes. Look with the eyes of your heart. Isn't there some time and place for you to hide away with God? Where and when?

If you're in college, agree with your roommate to have a quiet time each day or to post a sign on the door, alerting each other to the "holy place" time going on inside.

If you're a new mother, consider using all that time in the rocker as power time with God.

If you're a young mother with lots of little ones, consider going to bed with them and waking at midnight for an

like, "Oh God, it's so early. Help!" I'm not kidding! Then I emotionally bow before Him and commit to a private rendezvous for later in the day. I usually spend my hour with Him in the later part of the morning, after the kids have left for school and my house is quiet. And yes, I do often blow it. But most days, this is my discipline.

I confess that, in part, I do this out of my hedonistic quest. I've discovered such pleasures in my time with God and, without fail, my day goes better when He gets the first part of it.

hour of holy solitude or, like me, hide in a wonderful bubble bath right after you put them in bed.

If you have a dog, start your time with God by talking to Him while you walk your furry friend, and then return home to light a candle and read your Bible.

If you have a long commute to work, get an audio Bible and spend half of the time listening to the Word and half of it singing praise songs and praying out loud.

If you have a chaotic schedule, start *scheduling* God into your planner during your lunch break.

Afraid there's no time to fix your life? No time to give solitude to God? Think again. Girl, you don't have the time *not* to start with God.

You're a woman of the new millennium; be creative. Not only will the day go more smoothly, but as time goes on, you'll have your true, unique, individual, God-appointed call for your life revealed to you in this quiet time.

Kairos: The Right Time

Speaking of time, the word *kairos* shows up in the Bible as *time*. Second Corinthians 6:2 reads, "I tell you that the 'right time' [*kairos*] is now, and the 'day of salvation' is now" (NCV). That's the apostle Paul writing, but I'm telling you that now is the time to find God—if not for the first time, to find Him again under all the chaos. You'll never get less busy.

Kairos is that moment when our beings radiate with honor and praise for God. The brilliance of the moment illuminates

God's existence. It's when we, in all our pitiful neediness, recognize Him.

It's that moment when you have absolute certainty that God *is*. Your spirit connects, not superficially but deeply. You cannot help but worship Him. You do not worship Him out of routine or duty but out of spontaneous emotion. It's like the shipwrecked swimmer who gains sight of the shore. Like the tiny human standing on the side of the Grand Canyon, who cannot stop her praise from erupting. Like the crazed woman with her feet in the sand, watching clams dance and enjoying God's rescue.

> Living spiritually requires something more than just not sinning or doing good works. In order to live in the kingdom of heaven, you must abide in me. Your identity is in me.[1]
> —from *The Sacred Romance* by Brent Curtis and John Eldredge

Perhaps the most profound biblical example of glory is found in the story of Moses in Exodus 33. The prophet actually has the guts to ask God to see His glory. God explains that Moses can't see it in fullness or he would die, but He does give the faithful man a glimpse of it. God passes by Moses, covering him with His hand so the fullness of His own glory doesn't blow Moses away.

When Moses comes down off of the mountain, the radiance is still hovering over him visibly. Aaron and the others are scared silly to come near Moses. The glory of God is that magnificent. Moses appeases them by covering his face with a veil, but they do not doubt . . . not for one second . . . that this man was *with* God.

How did you get this ability to glorify God? By being with Him.

9-1-1 Glory

My son, Robby, was an adorable four-year-old when he learned about 9-1-1 at preschool. He thought he'd check it out that night right before I gave him a bath. Was I embarrassed when an officer of the law showed up at my house! The police officer waited while I got Robby from the bathtub so the little guy could see that, in fact, an officer does come if you call.

I'm sure it happens a lot. Little fingers test the system.

Not this time.

Not Anthony Sutko.

"My daddy killed me with a knife," he matter-of-factly stated to the 9-1-1 operator.

The eight-year-old went on to explain that his daddy had stabbed his mother to death and then had turned the knife onto him. And, so he had.

Now recovering from his six stab wounds and living with a relative, Anthony was recounting his story on national television.

"God told me to play dead," says the boy.

> "Open the eyes of my heart, Lord. Open the eyes of my heart. I want to see You. I want to see You."

In the midst of being stabbed, the boy heard a voice. Though every human response would be to give in to the fight-or-flight mechanism built deeply within us, this boy didn't. He just suddenly lay still. And his father left.

How did he get to the phone with six gaping wounds in his body? "[God] sent His angel," said the boy almost as if he was surprised the question had to be asked. "The angel carried me to dial 9-1-1."

As the interview ends, Anthony is singing: "Open the eyes of my heart, Lord. Open the eyes of my heart. I want to see You. I want to see You." He doesn't miss one word. He lifts his voice high to the heavens and sings his little heart out.

And the country cries. Not just *for* Anthony—though there is so much of that mixed into the tears—but *because* of Anthony. This is his moment of glory in the deepest spiritual sense. In the face of the most horrid tragedy . . . in this moment, in this place, in this *time* (kairos) . . . he is radiant.

It seems to me that a lot of us live our lives in 9-1-1 mode. While we don't have heartbreaking tragedy to report, we're certainly crying out for help. Financially, emotionally, spiritually. Some of us even walk around whining about how hard life is.

Maybe, just maybe, it's time to stop fearing that we'll never have the time to get things on track and to make this moment of chaos our *kairos*—our time to glorify God, *especially* if there really has been some 9-1-1 crisis in your life. And *extra especially* if that 9-1-1 crisis was caused by your own foolishness. You see, sometimes it is the place of our foolishness that God desires most to show Himself to this world through His goodness and His power to rescue. Sadly, that's often the place we fear most being used.

Afraid of your past? Oh baby, is the next chapter just for you!

Making It Work

At the right time [kairos], I heard your prayers . . .
I tell you that the "right time" [kairos] is now.

—2 Corinthians 6:2 NCV

Take it from this nighthawk—writing to you at 11:28 PM and going strong—sometimes mornings are not the very best part of your day. I try to begin my day in prayer, but then I set aside a time that's more productive for me to sink into the presence of God. As you meditate on 2 Corinthians 6:2, don't ask God *if* you should start to schedule daily time to be with Him. Rather, ask Him *when* it should be. Where should it be? Will you need an iPod for worship music? A candle for the quieting of your heart? (A lock on the door to keep the kids and four-footed critters out?) How much of your day should you schedule with Him? Today your journaling assignment is to write your own personal goals for setting aside time to be with God.

5

Fear #4: My Past Disqualifies Me

As I made it a priority to spend time with God, He was making big changes. I didn't have it all figured out, but I knew one thing: He was taking parts of my life that I'd long pretended didn't hurt, and He was allowing me to feel them as if for the first time. And though His touch was often like that of a physician touching a fresh wound, the pain was always fruitful. He was healing me.

And He was regularly inviting me to take off my previously treasured mask of perfection to allow others to see the evidence of healing from His amazing touch.

It wasn't everyone who needed to see these secret places. It wasn't just anyone who got to see them. Often it was a friend who'd stuffed a similar sin deep down into her own secret place. At other moments it was a teenage girl who was facing the same dilemma I'd faced when I was her age. Each time I shared my story of how God was slowly healing me, I gained confidence that I wasn't alone. Many in the body of Christ were hurting. It was clear that if God was going to direct my life, my sinful past was going to be a big part of my future.

I decided to set aside one week to fast and pray, asking the Lord for clear guidance about how to proceed. I specifically wanted to know if I should write a book about my experience. I told no one. Me write a book? More ridiculous still, me write a book on sexual purity? Surely I was off course. After all, I wasn't the poster child for abstinence.

"Lord, do You want me to write a book?" I asked each day. Little signs came one at a time whispering, "Yes." Scripture verses. Circumstances. But nothing could have prepared me for God's big finale.

I was at a community festival, enjoying my children, when I saw a woman running toward me with great intention. I knew her. She was a previous employee of ours who'd left under extremely bitter circumstances and usually snubbed us in public.

"Oh, Lord," I thought, fearing her intentions. "There's going to be a big show in town tonight! Help!"

But when she got to me, she gave me a warm welcome and simply said, "Hey, Dannah, I heard you're working less than you used to."

"Yeah," I answered dumbfounded.

"Great, then you can write that book I've always thought you should write," she bubbled!

"You think I should write a book?" I asked.

"Yes, I've always thought that," she answered. "I thought I'd told you before. You should definitely write a book."

With that, she got distracted and wandered off. I stood there not knowing whether to cry or to shout.

Either would have been an appropriate expression of my overwhelming amazement at God's kindness.

God is calling me to write a book, I wondered.

Wait a minute. Another thought fueled with fear rolled through my head. God is calling me to write a book!

Did I have the guts to be that transparent? Only a handful of people knew about my past. How would I ever endure the process of being public about my past?

———

Stop running from the past. In that very place may be the seed of your greatest call. It has been for me. Despite ten years of living under the weight of fear that my past disqualified me,

God has chosen my deepest moments of sin—and His amazing ability to rescue and restore me—to glorify Him. Have you, too, been held back by the paralyzing fear that your past disqualifies you?

Prequalified to Glorify God

Is there a place of sin in your past that still hurts to talk about? A divorce? An abortion? Alcoholism? Debt?

Perhaps it's not your own sin but the sin of someone close to you that has veiled your hope to glorify God in wounds still seeping with unforgiveness. Your husband's battle with pornography? Your dad's incestuous touches? The judgment of a congregation?

It doesn't have to be a sin at all, but it could be deep pain that cripples you in your quest to pursue God's purpose for your life. Cancer? Infertility? The failure of a business? The loss of a child? Or, even sadder, the fear that your sheltered past is relatively irrelevant to where people are today? Oh, how sad when a clean testimony feels like no testimony at all.

The fear of our past is so big that I've written an entire book about it called *The Secret of the Lord*. We simply

Overcoming the fear that your past disqualifies you is one of the most challenging tasks of pursuing your life's purpose. I unfold the journey step-by-step in a book entitled The Secret of the Lord. *Did you know that 50 percent of women in church are still looking for one close friend with whom to share their deepest secrets? Look no further, my friend. God knows your secret. He wants to tell you His.*

cannot let our fear of the past disqualify us from glorifying God. When it is yielded to him, it is often the very thing that qualifies us.

The primary purpose of Christ's life and death was to rescue us. The Bible says that "the Son of Man came to find lost people and save them" (Luke 19:10 NCV). The Greek word for *save* in this verse is a word that means *to be healed* or *made whole*. Being saved from sin isn't just knowledge in your head that you're forgiven. It's a total saturation of wholeness in your life. This complete healing renders us incapable of hiding it because we are in awe of God's powerful touch. Anything short of that is not the full salvation . . . the complete healing.

A Legacy of Healing

Though I've never spoken to her and she keeps her private life very quiet, I see the legacy of healing in Amy Grant. I still remember sitting on my bed in the '80s, dressed, I'm certain, in an oversized sweater and leg warmers, listening as Amy's voice crooned out of my very own record player. (Now, that does date me, doesn't it?) I listened to "My Father's Eyes" over and over again.

I watched Amy birth the Christian music genre almost single-handedly, marry young, start a family, and eventually explode into the pop culture. The whole world was watching her.

And then, we watched her divorce.

But not really. We didn't see the lonely nights of tears. Didn't hear how the couple expressed their anger. Were not privy to the hours spent in counseling during sixteen years of trying. To this day, we don't really know what happened—how much pain she knew. How much healing she needed. Grant's healing is as private as the divorce, but she's offered glimpses of it. She recalls sitting in a Sunday night worship program at Gospel Music Week after the divorce: "We're singing songs about mercy and forgiveness and healing, and in a very quiet way because I'm not really an outward person, I just said, 'I know this stuff is true. I know mercy is true, I know what forgiveness tastes like.'"[1]

> Being saved from sin isn't just knowledge in your head that you're forgiven. It's a total saturation of wholeness in your life. Anything short of that is not the full salvation . . . the complete healing.

Apparently, there was a return—a fresh infusion of God's grace, if you will—during her recording of *Legacy*, in which she brought faithful hymns to life: "Doing this hymns record, at every turn I was surprised by realizing this is where I came from . . . I had nearly forgotten . . . This is MY heritage! This is my history!"[2]

A moment of poignant healing came as she gave voice to the words of "My Jesus I Love Thee."

> I remember singing it as a kid . . . "*I love Thee because Thou hast first loved me and purchased my pardon, on Calvary's tree*," which by the way, even at seven years old, I knew that I had been purchased with the blood of Jesus. Those hymns do a pretty heavy thing in the mind of a kid . . . when it came for the time for me to sing that third verse, I just got so choked up time and time and time again. We had to keep rolling the tape back because it was "*In mansions of glory and endless delight. I'll ever adore Thee in heaven so bright. I'll sing with the glittering crown on my brow*," and that picture juxtaposed with public shame is so powerful. It was just my undoing. I probably think that was the greatest moment of healing for me, in the context of that album

. . . ridiculously outlandish mercy and love and forgiveness were not wasted on this forty-one-year-old woman.[3]

From what I've read, I don't think Amy would encourage or condone divorce any more than I would encourage or condone teen sex. What is courageous about this woman of faith is that rather than running from the legacy of her faith because of her sin, she is returning to it more powerfully. The healing she's received is one she passes on. She's allowed mercy to come to life through her healing.

Second Corinthians 1:3–4 tells us that "God is the Father who is full of mercy and all comfort. He comforts us every time we have trouble, so when others have trouble, we can comfort them with the same comfort God gives us" (NCV). Why did He rescue you? So you can pass the rescue on to someone else.

Your past does not disqualify you. In fact, it is the rescue from that past that qualifies you to pass on the healing.

Covenant Truth

Well, I can just hear a few feathers ruffling. I hope they're not yours. Let's just assume they're from that woman at church who looks like the church lady. She's pursing her lips and getting ready to say, "But you've forgotten that sin has consequences."

No, I haven't. In fact, I've lived with many of them. My consequences have included fear of pregnancy and disease during the season of my sin. After I got out of the relationship, I feared I might fall in love with a man who would not forgive me. (He did forgive me, and he is my hero!) I endured ten years of loneliness while I lived under the fear that God could not use me because of my sin. I've endured periods of sexual dysfunction in my marriage and vivid mental pictures of my sin that simply break my heart. I still occasionally endure judgment from people who can't see the deep work of repentance that God's done in my life. The consequence of my sin is that if I allow it to be seen so others can be healed and challenged to follow a different path, some will see only the sin and not the glory.

I can't measure my life by what other people think. The measure of my life's value will ultimately be determined by God. Our God is a covenant God. We enter into His covenant when we confess with our mouths that we have sinned and that Jesus is the sacrifice for that sin. There has to be a blood sacrifice to seal a covenant. Jesus is that sacrifice. At the moment of our confession, we enter into God's family through Christ's covenant.

Author Scott Hahn writes, "If God's covenant makes us His family, then sin means more than a broken law. It means broken lives and a broken home."[4] Sin doesn't remove us from God's family any more than a catfight between sisters at Thanksgiving dinner makes them less sisters. But sin does remove the blessing of family. Just as the sisters cannot revel in the blessing of one another's support, laughter, wisdom, and friendship, through sin we lose the blessings of God's defense and provision, joy, spiritual guidance, and sense of closeness. There are consequences when the covenant is broken by a pattern of sin.

The truth of this consequence is why I daily attempt to lead precious teen girls to choose a life of purity. It's why I'll resist my good friend's divorce until there's no other choice than to begin to help her heal. It's why I advise young couples not to enter freely into a life of irresponsible spending and debt accumulation. Sin hurts. If I don't call it sin, there is no truth in me. But the consequences of our sin do not include never being able to be used by God. The wonder of the covenant is that I can embrace both the truth that God can use my past for His glory and the truth that sin has consequences.

A Fugitive for God's Glory

Perhaps no one has known both the consequences of sin and the glory of being used by God quite like Moses.

He was like Kate on the hit TV show *Lost*. A fugitive.

It hadn't always been like this. Sleeping in the wilderness. Hoping no one would find out. And if they did, hoping they didn't ask. No, it wasn't always like this.

He'd once lived a life of privilege. Not anymore. Not since that day. In a fit of rage, he'd gone from prince to murderer. With one blood-letting blow his life had changed.

Someone saw. So, he ran. Destined to a life of hiding.

The irony of it is that decades later, God chased him down. *I am sending you,* God announced.

"Not me," he cried. But to no avail.

> When God gets ready for you to take a new step or direction in His activity, it will always be in sequence with what He already has been doing in your life. He builds character in an orderly fashion with a divine purpose in mind.[5]
> —from *Experiencing God* by Henry Blackaby and Claude V. King

God pursued a continuing love relationship with Moses that was real and personal. As a result, this fugitive murderer returned to the economic power center of the world, Egypt, and the city was undone. About two million unpaid workers—God's people who were defended as a result of His covenant with them—were granted their freedom.

God used Moses-the-fugitive-murderer.

The Weight of Glory

Moses led the people for years, leaving Egypt behind in search for God's promised land. Then God's people became thirsty. Not for the first time but for the third time, as far as we know. Each time they're found whining like bratty kids. They want to go back to the place of their slavery as we often do when the quest for freedom becomes difficult. (But don't quit now. You'll miss the glory, girl!)

The first time the Israelites whined for water, God told Moses to put a piece of wood in a bitter water source, and it became sweet to drink. The second time, God told Moses to strike the rock with his staff—the one that had been an instrument of many miracles. The third time, God told Moses to take the staff and to simply speak to the rock. Perhaps the people just didn't get God's power. God wanted to show it in full force by having Moses do nothing more than speak to the rock. But Moses was angry. He lost his head. In frustration, he used his staff to strike the rock. And that was *his* undoing.

God tells him that the consequence will be that he cannot go into the promised land.

Harsh? Yes! But understand it wasn't for anger or for hitting the rock that Moses was being punished. It was for stealing God's glory. The people knew that Moses' staff was an instrument of miracles. They knew that God had performed many for them in the past. But in their hearts, they had forgotten. When Moses struck that rock, he got in the way of God's ability to show Himself to His people in a new way.

God punished Moses-the-glory-stealer.

Glory Stealers

I wonder how much glory we steal when we gag believers from showing the rough spots and wounds God has healed. Just last night after a basketball game, my husband, the founder of Grace Prep high school, met a woman who was a glory stealer. The guys had just blown away the competition when my husband was called aside by our coach.

"This woman wants to speak to you about Billy," he said.

Bob smiled. Billy is a new student. He came to us covered in tattoos and wearing black leather to offset a shirt that read "When hell is full, the dead will inherit the earth." He also came to us searching for God and, after just a few days, found Him in the person of Jesus Christ. We took him to one of our Pure Freedom youth events. We always lay out the truth of sin, heaven, hell, and Jesus at each event. Billy said he could not wait for that short talk to end. He knew he needed to respond to it. When it was over and we asked for anyone who wanted to follow Christ publicly for the first time to please stand, Billy shot up like a rocket.

This teenage boy is not the same. His astute mental inquiries of the Christian faith keep me grabbing for my Bible. His unashamed testimony challenges me to be vocal. His new, peaceful countenance calls me to praise God. He is glorifying God. It's some story. Oh, but I'm reveling in God's glory. It's so easy to do. Back to the glory stealer . . .

"I was just asking about *that* boy's tattoos," the woman said.

"What about them?" asked Bob.

"Well, they should be covered up," she stated emphatically.

"Hmmm. Well, I don't know if you know Billy's story, but . . ." Bob began.

"Yeah, your coach told me that he's new and he just got saved," she interrupted. She would go on to use the term "got saved" many times, promising that she really was happy about it, *but . . .*

You know the shtick: "It's a bad testimony." "*Someone else* might have a problem with it." "It could lead others to follow his example."

"I'm not discounting that he got saved or anything. It's just that his tattoos should be covered," she said.

"During a basketball game?" Bob asked. "When the rest of the team is wearing jerseys, you think he should wear something else?"

"Yes," she said. "I mean, it's great that he got saved and everything, *but . . .*"

She couldn't see it. Couldn't see the brilliance of Billy's face. She was missing the very beauty of this boy's rescue story. She was attempting to steal God's glory.

She walked off with her feathers ruffled.

I wonder how many kids stuck in the often spiritually dark goth lifestyle Billy will witness to because he's approachable to them? I wonder how many times those tattoos will open up conversations that lead to Christ? Billy's past, tattoos and all, can be the very place God uses to bring Himself glory.

Now, I know this tattoo thing is arguably a gray area. My husband's debater has every right to prefer that Christians not be imprinted with tattoos, as another may have to get a tattoo that says "Jesus Loves You!" Her shame comes in her attempt to hide and cover Billy's past, gagging him from sharing his unique rescue story.

She's a glory stealer.

Don't let glory stealers gag you from sharing your rescue story. And don't let your fear of them gag you either. Here's a well-kept secret: There simply aren't that many of them! They're just very vocal. Here's another: there's a tiny little bit of a glory stealer in all of us.

Not you?

Well then, you won't mind taking my little test. Here goes. As you read through this chapter in which I wrote of my consequences . . . shared Amy Grant's healing . . . unfolded Billy's story . . . was there any inkling of judgment in you? I mean, are you ready to let all three of us walk in His glory?

> "When the glory of God touches the ugliest part of your life and uses it, there is no pride. Only awe.
>
> —Dannah Gresh, *The Secret of the Lord* "

Let me invite you to live in His glory. It's complex. It's filled with the responsibility of truth. It'll scare you silly. But it'll take you one step closer to finding the freedom to live the life God designed for you.

Don't move on in this book until you take some time to really meditate at the end of this chapter. If you don't, you'll be walking on thin ice in the next chapter. The first four fears are well conquered in my life.

This last one, it's a doozy.

Making It Work

Praise be to the God and Father of our Lord Jesus Christ. God is the Father who is full of mercy and all comfort. He comforts us every time we have trouble, so when others have trouble, we can comfort them with the same comfort God gives us.

—2 Corinthians 1:3–4 NCV

What comfort has God given to you as you seek healing from hurts in the past? Journal about that, focusing on whether or not you are willing to pass on the comfort.

6

Fear #5: I'm Going to Fail

I couldn't believe I was here, sitting in a publisher's conference room. I felt a little outnumbered at the big table filled with a handful of kind but serious editors with important titles.

Publisher. Vice president. Acquisitions editor. Marketing director. Publicist. And then there was me.

I was pretty sure I was wearing a sign with a title that read "Still-slightly-overworked-young-mom-with-a-tad-too-ambitious-dream-of-becoming-an-author."

Stay cool, Dannah, *I said to myself as I glanced toward my husband. He sent me a* you're-doing-it *smile. The meeting was almost over, and I hadn't stuck my foot in my mouth. In fact, I'd been impressively composed, answering all the tough questions just as Bob and I had rehearsed.*

"Dannah," began the publisher, "I have just one more question for you. What goals do you have in terms of number of books you'd like to sell for this title?"

That was the one. The big question. We'd practiced that one multiple times.

I leave it to you as the experienced partner in this venture to establish credible, attainable goals. *I heard myself rehearsing the words in my head.*

But they didn't come out.

Instead, some flow of consciousness . . . an all-too-transparent naive expression of enthusiasm . . . an unrealistic dream came out of my mouth, like the wave of an ocean.

"Well, Elisabeth Elliot was my favorite author in my college years. She's sold something like 300,000 copies of Passion and Purity. *Surely, a more contemporary version of her classic would be able to sell at least that many. So 300,000 would be a good goal." I caught myself and stopped though there was more coming.*

The once pleasant faces began to stare at me in blank disbelief.

The quiet, awkward pause took my breath away.

"You know," began the vice president, in his kind, Southern accent, "most authors would be delighted to sell five thousand copies of a first book."

A burst of nervous laughter caught me in the chin as evidence that he was simply verbalizing what everyone else was thinking.

"In fact," he continued. "John Grisham did sell only five thousand of his first work. I think a . . ."

His long and kind education trailed off in my mind as I sank into my thoughts. Loser! You just blew it. What on earth were you thinking!

A few hours later, Bob was kindly picking me up off the floor in our Chicago hotel room.

I was sure it was the end of the road with this publisher.

———

Fear of failure. It's a whopper.

Can you identify? Do you know what it feels like to fear failure? It seems that once we come to terms with anything in our past, Satan rises up to convince us that all the mistakes we've made will resurface.

Now, don't be discouraged, but I think the best way to overcome this fear is with the truth that God *expects* you to fail.

Does that surprise you? He knows better than you do that you'll need a fresh start yet again. Why else would He warn you of it in Galatians 5:1?

The Snare

Galatians 5:1, offered in a letter addressed to *believers*, reads, "We have freedom now, because Christ made us free. So stand strong. Do not change and go back into . . . slavery" (NCV). God's just crying out to us to be aware—very aware—that we could lose ground.

Interestingly enough, the Greek wording contained in the warning to not "go back into slavery" gives us a vivid picture of how we most often lose our freedom. The wording is a common word for being trapped as if by a snare. Now, I know you're sitting there, 100 percent woman, and I'm sitting here all painted up in my *very* hot pink nail color, but let's just venture into the world of hunting, shall we?

> "We have freedom now, because Christ made us free. So stand strong. Do not change and go back into . . . slavery" (Gal. 5:1 NCV).

A snare isn't your typical steel foothold trap, which looks painful and nasty with its iron teeth. No, the snare is far more subtle looking. It's a simple piece of steel cable that forms a loop. It appears nonthreatening, if it is even noticed at all. When an animal walks though the snare, it walks calmly. It just keeps walking through it, feeling nothing. Soon it may feel a little tension, but it just plods on. As the animal feels greater tension, it pulls harder and presses forward. Soon its own force of movement has enslaved it to the snare. It doesn't realize that if only it had backed out earlier, it could have gotten away. By the time it recognizes that it's stuck, it's too late. The capture is subtle and is empowered *by the animal's own actions.*

What a vibrant picture. I don't know about you, but I never meant to become an overworked, underrested, overcommitted, underinspired woman with no freedom to pursue God's dream for my life. But twelve years ago, that's exactly where I was. If we are truthful, it's most often our own actions . . . our own decisions to move forward . . . our own quest to keep up with the Joneses that get us into such a place of bondage. Oh, certainly we alone are not to blame. The enemy set a subtle trap of expectations, responsibilities, and dreams. Once we've been in the snare, we never forget how it feels. And any familiar echo of the place in which we were first ensnared can cause the fear of failure to rise up.

I don't know about you, but I never meant to become an overworked, underrested, overcommitted, underinspired woman with no freedom to pursue God's dream for my life.

A Ragamuffin's Snare

U2's Bono reads his work. Rich Mullins named his band after his book, *The Ragamuffin Gospel.* Christian authors and psychologists turn to him. In the seventh decade of his life, the Roman Catholic author Brennan Manning bends the ear of evangelical leaders.

His spiritual journey began in my home state.

After 22 years of living by second hand faith on February 8, 1956, I met Jesus . . . It was noon. The Angelus bell from the cloistered Carmelite monastery sounded in the distance. I was kneeling in a small chapel in Loretto, Pennsylvania. At five minutes after three, I rose shakily from the floor, knowing that the greatest adventure of my life had just begun.[1]

The adventure had begun. And, like Moses, Manning led for many years without failure.

Then came the 1970s. And his snare. Alcoholism.

While he was ministering on a college campus in Florida, Manning discovered alcohol. He knew he was blowing it. He understood the foolishness of it. But he walked into the snare anyway.

After six months in treatment, Manning's ministering strength was not gone. Rather, it increased. He dipped into the treasure once again. This time he was able to comfort others he could not before. He brought with him God's healing from alcohol. Mask-free and ready to share God's rescue story, Manning became an author.

Until 1980. He walked back into the snare. He relapsed.

Again he walked through God's grace and healing. Soon he was strong once again, and he moved forward. He met and married Roslyn, and they served God side by side.

Until the '90s. He stepped into the same snare yet again. Empowered by his own movement, his own motions, his own desires . . . he relapsed.

Another journey through the depth of God's grace and healing. Another chance to try. Today, he is writing again. Passing on the healing.

If he did not rise up to recover after each ensnarement, he would be idolizing his sin rather than fighting to put God back onto the throne of his heart. When we make our sins our idols, they keep us from the treasure of God, exalting them and their power above Christ's power to cleanse. How do we know when we are idolizing our sin? This may be really politically incorrect, but I think a sure sign is that, instead of sins, we call them addictions.

Snares or Addictions?

A few years ago, ABC's John Stossel completed a compelling television piece on the term *addiction*. He interviewed Stephen Dewey of the National Institute on Drug Abuse, which calls drug addiction a "disease that will waste your brain." This is our government's official policy. And government-funded researchers like Dewey, of course, agree.

"Addiction is a disease that's characterized by a loss of control," said Dewey.

Stossel asked Dewey if he was suggesting that drug users don't have free will.

"That's correct," he said. "They actually lose their free will. It becomes so overwhelming."[2]

An alarm went off in my soul. No free will? *Doesn't the Bible say God won't tempt us beyond what we are able to bear?* I asked myself. I can certainly understand the pull, but I wondered if we aren't really just excusing sins of overdrinking, overworking, overeating, illicit sexuality, gossip, control, and other vices.

Do you ever fear that you'll fail? that you'll wander from Him once again? You've been down that road. Felt the failure.

I think our best defense against this fear is to realize that we are fully capable of failing and have been warned by God Himself to be careful or we'll lose our freedom once again. It's time to start calling sin what it is. And it's time to start watching for the snares that pull us back into it.

Society's Snares

Some snares are societal. Some fall for snares of food. Others, snares of entertainment. Mine is work. It soothes me. Maybe my true sin is love of the praise and acceptance that comes when a job is well done. Workaholism is, after all, the one "addiction" we honor. (You don't have to have a job to fall for this snare, by the way. I know a lot of moms who are professional volunteers, and their families pay for it. I know a lot of college students and even high-school students who don't know what it means to rest and who are existing on antidepressants because of the overload.)

For many years I've lived relatively free of my sin of over-working. I have some strategies in place to help. For example, I don't use a cell phone except to travel. Using one zaps me of my "holy space" with God. I become consumed with connecting to people and moving projects along rather than staying closely connected in conversation with my precious Lord. This boundary and some others have kept me enjoying my family and fulfilling my true purpose.

Just behind nurturing my relationship with God, I am called to be a supportive and faithful wife and an attentive and engaged mother.

You must understand that years ago, when I began saturating myself in God's presence, He clearly called me to place my husband and children right under Him on my priority list. That meant my vocational calling and volunteer work had to submit to the demands of my family. It was the primary reason I chose to work only part-time. Just behind nurturing my relationship with God, I am called to be a supportive and faithful wife and an attentive and engaged mother. This season of my life is saturated with hours of simply being available to my growing children. Though I've found boundaries to protect my family and me, the sin of overworking is a consideration every single day of my life.

Call it an addiction to work if you want, but it's better for me to call it what it is. Anything that takes me away from mothering during this season of my life is sin.

It's a snare.

Sinful Snares

Some snares aren't as acceptable. They are obvious, outright sin. Take, for example, sexual sin. Did you know that today in America, the porn industry is more lucrative than football, basketball, hockey, baseball, and Nascar combined? Did you know that while Hollywood puts out about four hundred movies a year, the porn industry releases seven hundred . . . a month? Did you know that approximately 65 percent of Christian leaders today admit they struggle with sexual compulsion of some type, mostly pornography? (Yes, I said Christian *leaders*!)

Don't be too comfy sitting there thinking it doesn't affect women. How did you like the movie *The Notebook*? Based on Nicholas Sparks's book, the story begins with an old man reading to an old woman with dementia and Alzheimer's. She recognizes no one. He's reading from a notebook that tells the story of two young lovers. As if the romantic twists and turns of the young lovers' story aren't enough, in the end the story is about the old couple. And, in the intoxication of the story, she remembers. She knows him. They die happy in each other's arms.

Oh, how we became caught up in it. (At least I did.)

Here's the problem. The two romantically directed sex scenes are socially common but not biblically acceptable. Married or not, anytime I fill my mind with anything sexual outside of my own marriage bed, it is sin. Ephesians 5:3 commands that you and I not allow even a "hint" of sexual sin into our lives. Do we "hint" at sin when we watch movies like *The Notebook*? I think we do.

It's a snare.

Intellectual Snares

In the apostle Paul's day, he faced tremendous intellectual snares. In fact, the stronghold of secular wisdom in Ephesus would eventually be evidenced by the world's third-largest library, the Library of Celsus, which housed up to fifteen thousand scrolls just a few decades after Paul ministered there. Ephesus wasn't offering the truth of God but the worldly thinking of the day, and it was hostile to God.

Sound similar to our educational centers of today? I guess a good place to start would be the schools that shape the intellectual foundation of our children.

Our hometown is home to Penn State University, so we get lots of great plays. Last week, *The Great Tennessee Monkey Trials*, the story of the John Scopes trial, was in town, so Bob and I took the entire student body of Grace Prep to see it. It was very fair, presenting both a strong Christian worldview and a secular humanist point of view. Afterward we took the students back to school to debrief. There we enjoyed a two-hour conversation that we resumed the next day as students defended their worldview and discussed teleology, fiat creationism, evolutionary creationism, the second law of thermodynamics, and other key issues. And we dug into God's Word as our standard of truth.

There were also a lot of public school buses at that play. My heart broke when I heard the teachers from those buses laughing at the Christian worldview. They hooted and hollered when the Christians in the play lost a point and jeered at difficult questions of faith. I wondered if the parents of those teachers' students knew how their faith was torn down that day by authorities they respect.

Sometimes our snares don't draw us in. More and more, we sit by and let them influence us. We allow them to pull us out of the intelligent debates and, thus, give them authority. That seems to be what's happening in our public schools and, especially, public universities. More and more, the Christian worldview is attacked by secular humanists. More and more, we pay to let them influence us.

It's a snare.

Financial Snares

Perhaps the most common snare is financial. It seems to me that a lot of us have jobs simply for one reason—to make money. I really think that's a pathetic distraction from God's purpose for your life. Now, don't get me wrong. You may need to work to provide for your family and even provide for the needs of others around you when God invites you to help. However, if you are in a career that you hate, but you do it just for the money, I believe you're missing God's best for you.

In order for God to birth freedom in my life, I had to walk away from the financial trap of living in debt. We sold our adorable little picture-perfect home and rented a pretty pathetic little house for three years. We sold our businesses, and when what was supposed to be a million-dollar deal went bad, we were faced with paying off about $60,000 personally. Of course, that's exactly when God called my husband out of the marketing business and into the development of Christian education. (Now, there's a high-paying career field for ya!)

> If you are in a career that you hate, but you do it just for the money, I believe you're missing God's best for you.

Ironically, while I was still just releasing my first book and Bob was in his first couple of years of a Christian-education salary, we paid that $60,000 off! I just have to stop to hoot and holler. You've got to understand what a miracle this was to us. We'd had a cash flow of up to two million dollars a year running through our little fists for nearly ten years and could *barely* make ends meet. We were weighed down and drained by the debt. Suddenly we were stripped of our community status as business owners and our cash-flowing monster. We were just one starving writer and a Christian school administrator making about $40,000 annually. Yet somehow we got entirely out of debt? What is up with that? God is so good!

I know so many who *hate* their jobs. They speak of the dread, the office politics, and the lack of adventure and purpose, but they stay for financial reasons. They stay shackled to their jobs. I can only say this because I've walked the path. While there was a point that I believe my years in the marketing world were ordinary moments preparing me for God's perfectly timed purpose, I also believe there came a point when it was wrong for me to stay in that place. I stayed far too long for . . . don't miss this . . . financial reasons.

It's a snare.

So Stand Strong

We've not begun to look at the five little questions that reveal the life God designed for you, but we have covered some significant territory as we tear down the untruthful fears that keep us from pursuing an adventuresome life. You can't even begin to live in your God-designed life until you are free from these fears. And freedom comes from staring them right in the eye and admitting that they exist. Then you fight them. Could you fail? Well, God doesn't call you to freedom so that you can cycle right back into enslavement, but it is a very real threat. If it were not, God wouldn't warn you of it.

Galatians 5:1 encourages us to "stand strong" so we won't get caught up in slavery. Think of it in terms of warfare intelligence. Call sin what it is. Sin. And be prepared to readjust your life to step out of your snares. Carefully analyze your life regularly to see if you've been walking into a snare that you haven't yet recognized.

In fact, that's what I'd like to do now. Let's analyze your life. Let's see if we can determine if you're standing in a snare of enslavement that keeps you from your God-designed appointment or if God is allowing you to feel some discomfort as a method of molding you for future assignments.

Roll up your sleeves with me. It's time to enter the battle to find the freedom from the fears so you can live in the life God designed for you.

Making It Work

We have freedom now, because Christ made us free. So stand strong. Do not change and go back into the slavery of the law.

—Galatians 5:1 NCV

What kind of snare can realistically raise up fear of failure in you? Societal? Sinful? Intellectual? Financial? As you meditate on Galatians 5:1, ask God to show you a picture of where you may currently be ensnared. Write about it in your journal.

PART TWO

FINDING THE FREEDOM TO LIVE THE
LIFE GOD DESIGNED FOR YOU

"That's the big picture, isn't it? The big realms are slugging it
out. We're just the meat in the sandwich. And for some reason,
we're worth it.

I don't know why, but we are."

—Mel Gibson on belief in the supernatural

God's Battle Plan for Freedom

Picking up the pieces that were left of me after my first publisher's meeting, Bob had taken me out for my first taste of what would become a Chicago favorite, Giordano's pizza and root beer. My belly full and my ego worn, we walked through the windy streets.

"God, what am I doing here?" I whispered under my breath, feeling the taunting of a spirit of failure. I wished I could just fast-forward and be past this humiliation.

Your mission is . . . I felt God's voice booming passion into my heart as words simply unfolded in my mind. A clear and concise mission statement. An answer to the question. Words of affirmation.

I would never forget them.

It would never take any effort to recall them.

In the face of the fear of failure, God emblazoned His call on my life as clearly as if there had been a burning bush brightening the streets of the city.

The fear of failure didn't slink off quickly, but a battle began to rise up over my life as I began to see the life God designed for me.

My obedience to God in the face of my fears would determine who would become the victor.

What is freedom? It's defined as "the absence of restraint in choice or action" or "not being unduly hampered or frustrated." In the context of our quest together, the definition would be "the absence of restraint in choice or action *to pursue the life God designed for you*" or "not being unduly hampered or frustrated *in the pursuit of the life God designed for you.*"

Do your circumstances and responsibilities restrain your choices and actions in pursuing the life God designed for you? Are you ensnared? or *just* discouraged? You see, discouragement or feeling a tad unfocused in your pursuit of God's purpose doesn't *necessarily* mean you are ensnared. There may be times when God allows discouragement as a form of molding your character. During these times, the pursuit of freedom is best engaged by staying in the place where God has you. However, there are other times when you're ensnared and it is time to pursue freedom by moving on.

You cannot move forward in your pursuit of a God-designed life until you have identified which situation you are facing. I can help. But to accurately assess where you are, we must begin in this battle for freedom with a plumbline for what a God-designed life looks like.

Let me give you a fresh reminder of what freedom does in our lives.

C. S. Lewis vs. Sigmund Freud

They need no introductions.

Yet at first glance, it may seem as though the names of C. S. Lewis and Sigmund Freud don't go together. One is quickly associated with children's books, the other with psychology. But these two have so much in common, and they are together the perfect jumping-off point for our fight for freedom.

Both Freud and Lewis started their public lives much the same way. They were brilliant minds who were highly critical of others. They both admitted to clinical depression, pessimism, and a gloomy spirit. They both were very hostile toward their fathers, whom they blamed for shaping them negatively. They both had negative childhood experiences. Lewis's included the death of his mother at an early age. They both despised authority, especially what they perceived to be the foolish notion of an Ultimate Authority or God. These two lives seemed to be headed down a similar path.[1]

What Is Freedom?

"the absence of restraint in choice or action *to pursue the life God designed for you*" or "not being unduly hampered or frustrated *in the pursuit of the life God designed for you*"

Then in his early thirties, Lewis, a proclaimed atheist, observed a quality in Christians that was missing in his own life. One noted believer and close friend of Lewis's who had this quality was J. R. R. Tolkien, who later authored *The Lord of the Rings*. At a dinner with Tolkien and another Christian man, Lewis began to open his mind to God. He went on to read the New Testament in Greek. (Oh, to be so smart!) It made sense to him. He soon embraced the notion that he was a sinner. He surrendered himself to become a follower of Jesus Christ. But that's only the beginning. What God did in this man's life is amazing!

Those who knew Lewis before and after noted that he was entirely different. He suddenly began to develop close, happy friendships. He became outgoing. He came to love and value people, saying he realized they would go on long after other things had passed away. He no longer struggled with depression. He went on to marry in his fifties and had a fulfilling sexual life.

He wrote that he and his wife, Joy, "feasted on love every mode of it . . . No cranny of heart or body remained unsatisfied."[2] He was known for enjoying the little pleasures of watching a sunset or taking a bubble bath. He sought pleasure in a healthy way.

Freud never recovered from his existential despair. He never went on to have satisfying, close personal relationships, though he did seem to be somewhat well adjusted in his family. He felt that pleasure is equal to instinctual gratification and sexual fulfillment, and since that only happens periodically, it wasn't likely for humans to be happy. He had a frustrated sexual life in marriage, stating that by the age of thirty-seven he was "living in abstinence."[3] Toward the end of his career, he became angry that he was not recognized more and did not receive more awards and honors. When he began the long, painful journey of dying of cancer, he chose to die of a lethal injection that his physician administered at his request.

Lewis—as a Christian—found freedom.

Freud—as an atheist—never did.

Christianity vs. Atheism: Who Is Really Free?

The comparison of Lewis and Freud is not an isolated example. Living according to God's purpose and plan *does* result in greater happiness, according to a Barna survey. Eighty-four percent of those who both consider themselves Christians and say they live as closely to the standards of the Bible as possible are happy with their lives. This drops to only 67 percent among those who consider themselves Christians but admit they don't really know much about how to live according to the standards of the Bible. Get this! Happiness drops to 57 percent among those who consider themselves to be atheists. Those most likely to seek humanistic freedom find themselves least happy.[4]

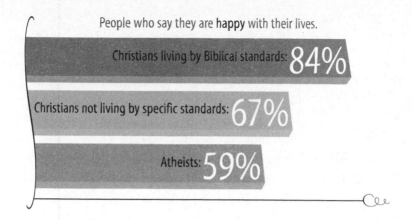

I think that the extraordinary difference in the lives of Lewis and Freud combined with stats like these merit a closer look. What was the primary difference in these two great minds who started life so similarly? Where did their paths diverge? It seems clear to me. Freud never embraced the language of sin. He replaced it with terms like *ego*, *repression*, *projection*, and *sibling rivalry*. Thanks to him, we are likely to excuse sinful adult behaviors by associating them with issues of childhood trauma. I'm not saying Freud wasn't onto something here. He was. We're certainly shaped in part by our childhood experiences. However, in over-emphasizing the power of those experiences in our lives and allowing them to be excuses for harmful behavior, he removed the language of sin. And in removing it, he allowed for a kind of unrestrained living that is a counterfeit for true freedom.

Sin is *the* battleground for your freedom to discover the life God designed for you. I simply cannot find a pathway out of the chaos without walking down a road that carefully describes this word. Romans 3:23–24 reads, "All have sinned and fall short of the glory of God, and are justified freely by his grace through the redemption that came by Christ Jesus." There is no way to freedom without a stronger and more learned vocabulary of sin.

Author Anne Ortlund says, "Sin is such a big part of what God's word has to say to you that to ignore it would be to ignore God."[5]

Chata: *Missing the Mark*

The main Old Testament root word for sin is *chata* or *hatta*. It was an archer's term, which meant "to miss the mark." Now, if you were a skilled Hebrew marksman, what would you consider the mark of a target? The bull's-eye! You wouldn't want to settle for anything less. That's the intended purpose of your arrow. So this Hebrew word for sin means "to miss the bull's-eye." The bull's-eye is the life God designed for you. Did you get that? Read it again. The bull's-eye is the life God designed for you. God has a specific plan and purpose for your life, and anything that misses it is sin.

> The main Old Testament root word for sin is *chata* or *hatta*. It was an archer's term, which meant "to miss the mark."

It's so easy to see sin when we see someone *else* miss the target altogether. If someone commits murder, very few of us disagree that this is wrong. It's clearly sin. Think of some other clear examples of missing the entire target and add them to the diagram by labeling the arrows.

Maybe you've missed the target big-time. Maybe you're still trying to figure out how to heal from the abortion you chose to have. Maybe you're struggling with whether to confess a sexual affair. Maybe you've struggled with alcoholism. If so, let me remind you that I, too, have missed the target altogether. You're not alone. I promise you that I have some healing for you.

But first, let's get the fullest meaning of our all-important word. The meaning of chata doesn't simply imply that we've missed the target. It says we missed the *mark*—the dead center of the target—the bull's-eye. We often don't even perceive these "little" sins in our lives.

For example, when you pick out a skirt that's a little short and flirty and you have an extrasensual feeling when you wear it, you've missed the bull's-eye. You haven't missed the target altogether by having sex with a man who's not your husband, but you haven't hit God's mark for sexual purity either.

Let's bring this closer to home. Ever have a moment of good, old-fashioned, woman-of-the-household manipulation? One of those times when you tell the kids, "Oh, just don't tell your father!" Or when you just "forget" to tell your husband about the big credit charge at Pier One? We are so good at rationalizing manipulation. We often argue in our minds that it is for the best as we're keeping the peace. Ah, but have we "missed the mark" of trusting God, showing respect to our husbands, and being honest? You bet we have! Can you label the arrows with a few other sins that are harder to perceive but that we find ourselves in regularly?

The Mark

I don't want to be overly focused on the negative part of sin. There's a place for that in our definition, but the word *sin* isn't about what we're *not* supposed to be. It's about what we *are* supposed to be.

God is our maker. As our maker, He knows how we function best. He knows what works and what does not. He knows what's best for us. Hitting the mark allows us to experience God's best for our lives. In fact, in the Greek New Testament, the word for sin is *hamartano*, which means "to miss the mark and so not share in the prize." I think God was just getting exhausted with our misunderstanding of chatta, so He hit us in the head with what really matters in the definition in the New Testament word. The prize! The prize of living according to God's truth is the indescribable blessings He'll pour into your life when you obey Him.

Not seeing too many examples of Christians who seem to have such blessed prizes in their lives? I heartily agree with you. We're not living that differently from the world, so we're really not living in a place of freedom. In fact, reportedly only 7 percent of Christians claim to consistently attempt to live according to God's standards . . . His design.[6]

This is not for the fainthearted. If you enter the battle for freedom, you'll be in the minority. So many are satisfied to live with dissatisfaction. Oh, I'm sitting here, my nails painted a daring shade of OPI "It's All Greek to Me," my hair pulled up into a floofy knot with rhinestone clasps, my silver earrings dripping toward my shoulders, and my makeup just so. (Pardon the T-shirt. It's an at-home day.) I'm a girl's girl who loves chick flicks and bubble baths, but I'm also a warrior.

I've fought the battle.

I've found freedom.

> "Sin ... blocks contact between the natural and spiritual worlds. Sin introduces a kind of static interference in communication with God and as a result shuts us off from the very resources we need to combat it.[7]
> —Phillip Yancey

I've raised my bow, and I'm aiming for the mark.

The first step in aiming for the mark is to determine exactly where you are. Are you ensnared by anything that inhibits or restrains you in your pursuit of God's best? The next few chapters are short and sweet, but they'll help you to determine where you are and exactly what the next step is in your pursuit of freedom.

Making It Work

All have sinned and fall short of the glory of God, and are justified freely by his grace through the redemption that came by Christ Jesus.

—Romans 3:23–24

Have you had an incomplete definition of sin in your mind? It was OK before, but now God is calling you to a meatier knowledge, a more complete understanding, so that you can live the life He designed for you. Today in your journal write to God about how your view of sin has been challenged by this chapter. Ask Him what He wants you to do with that.

The Fishy Business of Snares

"Sell my home, Lord? But why?" I pleaded.

It had been several months since I'd gotten my first book con-
tract—and from the very publisher who'd seen the wide-eyed
enthusiasm that left me fearing failure. I spent a lot of days feeling
caught in the middle: halfway between my old life of overworked
chaos and my new passion to follow God's call on my life. Somehow
I had to help Bob manage the businesses that I was no longer a significant part of, effectively mother Robby and Lexi, and write a
book that could match the sales of my role model, Elisabeth Elliot.
(Ha!) At times I felt overwhelmed by the clean-up work God was
doing in my debt-ridden life.

As I pulled into my driveway, I pulled myself together and
walked into the house to find my husband sitting in the living room,
just staring into space. He looked stunned.

"What's wrong?" I asked.

"Well," he began softly. "I don't know how to tell you this, but
today at lunch I think God told me to sell our house."

Tears flowed.

Debt was a huge sin in our lives, and it strangled God's purpose
and potential right out of us. Yet we clung to our stuff like babies
crying territorially over their beloved toys. We had no freedom to
follow God's call. We were slaves to the debt and the house, the Jet
Skis, the nice cars . . . they were all part of our bondage.

Yet we loved them.

I walked onto the back deck and looked over a backyard of memories. Robby's sky fort complete with the addition he and my dad had built for baby Lexi. The pool with the wrap-around deck. The wonderful row of trees that Robby had climbed countless times . . . and had fallen from nearly as many. The flower bed that had won "yard of the month" and which had been Lexi's muddy sand- box. The water hoses and buckets and guns that had ignited fre- quent family water fights.

"Oh, Lord," I said. "If You really want us to sell this, please tell me You'll take care of my kids. This is going to break their hearts."

I slept hard that night and awoke expectantly. Surely God was going to tell me it was just a test. We didn't really have to let go of this precious first home of ours.

I opened my Bible to read my daily chapter in Proverbs. And there was God's answer. In perfect finality in Proverbs 14:26, "He who fears the LORD has a secure fortress, and for his children it will be a refuge."

Dannah, God seemed to be whispering, Do you look to Me as your fortress or to this house? I will take care of those little ones. I will be their refuge. Obey Me.

I knew this wasn't going to be easy.

The apostle Peter's situation wasn't looking good.

It hadn't been very long since Jesus was crucified and raised from the dead . . . and not so long since Peter had denied Christ. Defeated and discouraged, believing he no longer has a place of importance in Christ's plan, Peter returns to the thing he is most familiar with . . . his fishing business.

Now, what does that sound like? (Hint: he went back to his snare!)

He's not catching so many fish though. That happens when we get snared. As good as we may have been someplace before, it just doesn't work to go back when God's design for our lives calls us to move on.

Jesus hunts Peter down. He's not going to let this guy miss his purpose.

After a fine divine catch of fish, Jesus eats with His friends and then turns to Simon Peter and asks, "Simon son of John, do you truly love me more than these?" (John 21:15). Here is where we have to look deeply to hear Christ's truth. What does He mean when He uses the word *these*? Bible scholars are divided. Some say he's asking, "Peter, do you love Me more than you love these other disciples?" A minority group says He was asking, "Peter, do you love Me more than this fishing business?"

The fish thing resonates with me. It's easy for me to understand wanting to cling to the familiar rather than walking out in freedom to claim God's purpose for my life. I've been there so many times.

My "Fish"

My fish was once a boyfriend God told me again and again I could not have because it would cost my heart dearly.

My fish was once my first little home, but we were in debt beyond belief, and God wanted me to be free from that.

My fish has been my title in a city social club, but God saw that I was too busy, and He wanted me to be free to enjoy my family and Him.

My fish has been my position as a marketing consultant, but He wanted me to be free to pursue His design for my life.

Each time I found another fish, I felt as if Jesus were asking me, "Dannah, do you love Me more than *these*?"

A fish is anything that you cling to when God is calling you to move on. It's something that restrains your choices and actions to pursue God. It's something that causes you to feel unduly hampered or frustrated in your pursuit of God. Are you clinging to a fish? Is it a current job? a stubborn plan to launch something that God either isn't allowing to be launched at all or it's just not time yet? a relationship? Is it a fear or hurt you can't get past?

Three times Jesus asks Peter, "Do you love Me more than these?" Each time Peter says, "Sure, I love You." And Jesus says, "Feed My sheep!" He's *calling*. He wants the discouraged disciple to leave the fish behind, to leave the familiar . . . the secure . . . and to step out in freedom to follow Him.

Sometimes God allows us to be discouraged because He is calling us to redirect ourselves. The purpose of this discouragement is simple. God wants you to get miserable enough to recognize your fish. A fish is a snare that will strangle the life out of you, but you don't even know it. Snares are like that. Subtle. Not easily detected. If you are clinging to a fish, God is calling you to redirect your life.

So it was for Peter.

So it was for me. I thoroughly believe that the only way God could have helped me to recognize my fish was to allow me to become so discouraged and exhausted that it turned into physical depression. It was the kindness of God in this place of deep discouragement that led me to hope for a new calling.

Big Fish

The great missionary David Livingstone had a precious fish to love. He was a poverty-stricken young man with a dream to be a missionary to China. He sacrificed diligently to become a doctor and an ordained minister, working in between years of higher education to pay for his schooling. It took years, but he did it. He was finally about to grab out for that wonderful big dream, but alas, it was to God a squirmy, slimy fish. And suddenly the doors to China were closed tightly. Livingstone mourned the death of a precious dream.

But God had a bigger plan. Livingstone could have continued to hold on to that smelly fish, but all the while it would have been decaying as God wasn't about to open those doors anytime soon. Or he could watch to see where God was at work.

He watched.

He recognized that God was redirecting him.

And today Livingstone is credited as being the first significant missionary to bring the truth of Jesus Christ to inner Africa. He had amazing adventures there. Discovering Victoria Falls. Fellowshipping with untouched ancient native tribes. Wrestling with lions. Africa was God's perfect place of freedom and purpose for Livingstone. Always was. From before the world was created. From before Livingstone ever desired to be a missionary. Even during every moment he dreamed of China. God chose him to be a pioneer for the gospel in the wild and wonderful land of Africa. Would Africa know Jesus if Livingstone had not let go of something he loved?

The first thing you must discover is whether or not there is something God is asking you to adjust in your life. You cannot move forward toward your purpose without making sure it is the right one.

My friend, when you let go of the fish in your life, God takes care of *all* of your needs. (Of course, He does this in His perfect timing. You may have a few lessons to learn along the way. I did.) Are you discouraged or depressed? The first thing you must discover is whether or not there is something God is asking you to adjust in your life. You cannot move forward toward your purpose without making sure it is the right one. Sometimes to help redirect you, God will allow you to feel the discouragement of holding on to stinky, smelly fish!

Ephesians 5:17 says, "Do not be foolish but learn what the Lord wants you to do" (NCV). What a sad, foolish thing it would have been for Peter to continue to be a fisherman when God wanted to make him "the rock." How foolish it would have been for Livingstone to sit for years, waiting for China to open its doors when God wanted him to be *the* pioneering missionary of Africa! Instead of being fools, they learned what the Lord wanted them to do, and they did it.

Are you a bit discouraged? A lot discouraged? Stop. Ask yourself this question, "Is there anything that I'm holding on to?" Is there a snare in your life that smells a lot like a fish?

For me and for my husband, this point of identifying a battle plan for freedom to pursue God's call meant addressing the problem of debt. We were not free to pursue God's design for our lives while we were ensnared by growing financial burdens and the accompanying stress. In addition to a lot of other things like Jet Skis and expensive cars, God prodded us to let go of our first little home.

The mere thought of it broke my heart. But missing out on God's adventure for my life seemed far more painful.

I needed to let my life answer the question: "Do I love Him more than these?"

Making It Work

"Do you truly love me more than these?"

—John 21:15

I first heard this teaching on fish from a traveling evangelist. He spoke at a small church of about forty in a town called St. James, Missouri. I don't recall his name, but he left an indelible imprint on my life with the message he spoke. I loved my fish at the time. Wouldn't give 'em up. He opened my eyes to see that, and I've not been the same since. It was the beginning of my battle to be free from life's snares. Have you any fish that God wants you to let go of? Journal about that today.

9

Letting Go of Your Fish

"Joyce." I listened from the kitchen table as Bob spoke into the phone for both of us. "Bob Gresh. We've decided to go through with the listing."

My heart sank.

Goodbye, little house, I thought to myself.

I knew that if it was truly God calling us to this, it would sell fast despite the fact that houses were taking nine to twelve months to sell in our market.

"No, we'd like to list it at the full price we initially presented to you, Joyce," said Bob as I stood up and walked over to the stove to refill my teacup.

"Yes, I understand you feel it's too high," he said, standing firm. "I know . . . yes . . . we do understand that."

He was taking some flack. We must have looked like schmucks to this seasoned realtor who was probably twice our age.

"Well, if we have to pull the price down after a year, we will," he said. "Yeah, we can come sign the papers today. OK. See you this afternoon."

We instinctively sank into each other's arms.

My nature to control and manipulate felt comforted by the fact that keeping our price high would probably mean our house would not sell for a year or so.

Nothing could have prepared me for how fast it all happened.

Well, how'd ya do in that last chapter?

Are you holding on to a fish?

If you see fish in your life, it's a sure sign that God is asking for you to throw the big one back in. It's time for action!

The Slow-Mo Throw

Now that we've established that we must throw that big fish back, let's talk about how. I'd much prefer you didn't slap someone on the head with a big old sailfish. Be careful. God would never ask you to do anything contrary to His Word. He calls you to honor your father and mother, submit to your boss, and respect authority. It took me years to move from where I was to where God wanted me to be so that I could do it in a way that honored God.

If you sense God calling you to get out of debt and you do so by claiming bankruptcy, you're probably not being a good example for Christ (Rom. 13:7–8). If you sense God calling you to quit your job and you do so without a plan to provide for your family or in such a way that you leave your boss hanging, you're not being a good steward, and God requires this of you (1 Peter 4:10). If you find yourself in a relationship that's wrong and you cut it off in an unkind manner, you're forgetting that loving one another is the second greatest command (Matt. 22:39).

My advice to you when you identify a fish is to take it slow. But be willing to take whatever action is necessary to throw that fish back.

I'm deeply inspired by the former counselor to President Bush, Karen Hughes. As his advisor, she helped the president write major speeches, shape policies, and communicate with international leaders. She even coauthored his autobiography. She was considered by many to be one of the most influential women in D.C. Of course, that power came at the cost of much time away from home and church, something she struggled with reconciling. She recognized that she was ensnared and, my, was it a big one! She resigned (no doubt that she did it properly) and for a time was hardly heard from. Where did she go? Home, to be a mom. Recently she said, "A life in which I don't have time to fulfill my responsibilities as a mom or grow as a Christian isn't a life God intends for me."[1]

> If you sense God calling you to get out of debt and you do so by claiming bankruptcy, you're probably not being a good example for Christ (Rom. 13:7–8).

Can you imagine your fish being the power and prestige of being one of the most powerful women in Washington, DC? Wow! I bet she warred it out within herself as she weighed the responsibility she had to the nation against her role as mom to Robert. But Karen was more obedient than some of us might be if we touched such power:

> I learned that sometimes there are jobs you can't do during a specific season in life. For me, working at the White House at that point in my son's life was something I couldn't do. I don't think that means you have to choose either family or career. You just have to be willing to examine the big picture at different points in your career.[2]

The secret to letting go of her fish was found in her relationship with Christ:

I think my faith in Christ gave me the strength and peace I needed to step away from my job. If my life had been about gaining power or position, I wouldn't have been able to leave it once I achieved it. But my worth isn't based on a title or a career. We're all equal in God's eyes and we're uniquely created and loved by him.[3]

After several years at home, where her main positions were that of mom to a high-school-aged son, Robert, and Sunday school teacher to a class of toddlers, God has opened the doors for Karen to move back into a new position of influence in Washington, DC. I'm excited for her. I wonder what all those ordinary moments back in Texas were preparing her for.

Ordinary Moments

In 1 Samuel 16, the prophet gets a pretty direct word from God about letting go of a big fish. That fish is the king of Israel: Saul. Saul is not living in the dead center of God's plan for his life, and the consequences for him will be grave. God begins to prepare Samuel to let go of the king he serves.

"How long will you mourn?" asks the Lord. "Fill your horn with oil and be on your way" (1 Sam. 16:1). Be on your way. (Now, that's probably what Karen Hughes heard God speak to her spirit. It's certainly what I heard when God asked me to sell my home.)

So Samuel goes off to find the next king. First Samuel 16 and 17 mark the most curious part of King David's life for me. They tell the story of how Samuel anointed young David as the eventual king and go on to give an account of his first public moment of victory. The passage starts out with a proclamation from God. "*I have chosen . . .*" says the God of the universe. God trusted His own handiwork and knew that several years before, He'd woven just the right substance into a little guy born to Jesse.

So Samuel heads off to Jesse's home to anoint God's chosen one. Upon inspection, Samuel passes by all seven of Jesse's first boys.

Boys who looked strong.

Boys who looked wise.

Boys who looked street tough.

Then (oh, this is my favorite part), Samuel asks if there isn't anyone else. What's Jesse's reply? "Oh, sure, but he's tending sheep." It's an everyday, ordinary job. Tending sheep! How can this little guy be the one?

Jesse brings David out of the field, and he is, in fact, the chosen one. Can you just imagine the discernment coursing through Samuel's body when David walks into his presence? Yep, this is the one.

He is small.

He is without much experience.

He is wide-eyed and innocent.

But Samuel anoints him. And then . . . David's dad sends him back to the fields. Wait a minute! Wasn't this guy just anointed *king*? Shouldn't he get a robe, a scepter, a bodyguard, a budget? Nope! David goes back to being *just* a shepherd.

Today you might hear,

"She's *just* a housewife . . ."

"She's *just* a college student . . ."

"She's *just* running car pool . . ."

"She's *just* retired . . ."

"She's *just* . . ."

Ordinary moments.

Moments when we're willing to be just what God wants us to be and nothing more. Moments when we wait for the right time to resign, move, sell, or change. Moments when we're willing to be humble and willingly serve where we are. These are the moments God uses to further develop those special strengths and capabilities.

Out there in the field, David was *just* tending sheep, but he was also becoming a mighty warrior. He was learning to defeat hungry lions. He was learning to be watchful. He was learning to be brave. He was learning to love and protect a helpless flock.

He was learning to be king.

God needed a new leader with compassion. One who could perhaps settle for the quiet task of shepherding while looking for the opportunities in it to use his special strengths and capabilities? David was willing. In fact, that willingness was just what would set the stage for David's first great public moment of victory. David's father asked him to take loaves of bread and roasted grain to his brothers who were on the battlefront. David was appointed a new job. He was going to be *just* the gofer. Another ordinary task.

All the while, he was poised to let go of the life that he knew.

Then came the moment. He suddenly saw the bull's-eye—the dead center of his God-designed purpose. His eye was set on the mark. Everything in him knew he was appointed to this Goliath. So he gathered five simple stones. He gave God credit and took aim. And he released not only his first stone but also his former life.

David's ordinary moments had been preparing him for this Goliath moment. Nothing else had ever been so easy to accomplish. He hit more than Goliath's forehead. He hit the mark—the dead center of God's purpose for him.

Oh, the ordinary moments I endured during my ten years in marketing. Things that were not exciting. I often struggled with a restless spirit—hungry for something more.

How many photo shoots did I manage? Enough to give me the skills to know how to do it for my books for teen and preteen girls today!

How many pages did I endure being cut to smithereens by clients who didn't like the copy? Enough to make me understand that when my editor gets this, together we'll cut and paste until it's a better book!

How many banks and retail chains did I do market research for? Enough to give me wisdom to do market research for a new book to see if you actually have the same needs in your life that I have known in mine!

And if I had to teach one more group of bank tellers or retail salespersons our S.M.I.L.E. customer service skills, I think it would've ripped the smile permanently from my bored-to-tears face. There seemed to be no purpose in it, but God was building my speaking skills! I *know* this. When I was in that ordinary place, God was molding my abilities for this appointment that I have today. God needed to place some chapters in my life that seemed ordinary but that He'd one day use as a foundation for extraordinary things.

If you find yourself holding on to the snare of a fish, prepare yourself to move. Know in your heart that you have to quit your job, change your major, start the process of adoption, or whatever God is calling you to do, but don't do it so fast that you miss the ordinary moments of strengthening that God has for you right here. Right now.

Anointed with Power

Temporarily staying in an ordinary place isn't easy. The Bible says that the day Samuel anointed David as king was the day he was fully equipped with power. First Samuel 16:13 reads, "So Samuel took the horn of oil and anointed him in the presence of his brothers, and *from that day on* the Spirit of the Lord came upon David in power (italics added)."

I believe that the moment you are aware of God's appointment is the moment God equips you with His power. It may not feel that way, but if He's telling you He wants you to do something, He obviously knows you're capable. You should too.

However, the moment of God's appointment is not necessarily the moment you are called to let go of everything you currently know and do. It is time to *poise* yourself to let go. Be ready to release the life you currently know in God's perfect timing.

You may not have all the pieces in place. (Another good reason to stick to the ordinary moments and simply poise yourself to obey when God says the time is right to move.) But you do have, from this day on, the power you need to do what He's calling you to do *when* He calls you to do it.

> The moment of God's appointment is not necessarily the moment you are called to let go of everything you currently know and do. It is time to *poise* yourself to let go.

Unfortunately, that power doesn't necessarily guarantee that you'll always *feel* empowered. Speaking of which, sometimes discouragement in our lives occurs when we are ensnared by something we need to let go of. But sometimes it comes as a result of being in the very center of the bull's-eye.

Let's take another look at King David's life so you can be

certain whether your pathway to freedom involves poising yourself for great change or simply embracing the place you are in.

Making It Work

"There is still the youngest," Jesse answered. "But he is tending the sheep."

—1 Samuel 16:11

Ordinary moments. Sometimes the best thing to do when we recognize God is calling us to make a big change is to embrace the ordinary moments. What is it that you need to embrace as you let go of your big fish? Journal about that today.

10

Snares Are Not Set in Caves

It was August 1. The 107-degree sun was melting us as we stood there, saying good-bye to our friends.

I couldn't believe this was happening so fast.

It had been less than three months since we'd listed our house. It had sold at full asking price in just a few weeks.

Not only had God asked us to sell our home, but He'd asked us to move back to my hometown, known as Happy Valley, and to rent a much smaller, much older, kind-of-falling-apart house.

It'll be just for a few months, *I thought to myself as we rolled out of Sycamore Drive.* Surely with my book coming out in a few months and Bob working, we can afford to buy a modest house in three. Yes, I can make it three months in that little shack.

I didn't realize it at the time, but I wasn't moving into just a little rental house.

I was moving into God's carefully designed cave.

Is all discouragement evidence that we're missing the mark? that we've been ensnared by sin in our lives? No, not all. Job, after all, whose discouragement was accompanied by incredible grief and loss, was righteous in God's eyes.

Sometimes discouragement is to be embraced. It *is* part of

God's design for your life. It is what God requires to develop your character—to equip you for your purpose. *God planned even this part of your calling.* When you come to this place of discouragement, don't poise yourself to move! Be still. Know that He is God.

What is the difference? Well, usually the second form of discouragement comes not because you're clinging to something but because you've been driven to a cave.

The Cave of Adullum

Remember David, the guy who was "just" a shepherd and "just" a gofer? Well, since we last peeked in on his life, he's been applauded for hitting Goliath between the eyes. He's risen from the role of shepherd and gofer to great and mighty warrior. In fact, the nation of Israel has been known to favor him over King Saul, shouting, "Saul has killed his thousands, but David his tens of thousands." This hasn't gone over so well with the self-absorbed king.

Soon Saul tells his son Jonathan and all the attendants to kill David. Jonathan warns David, and off he goes, fleeing for his life. He runs and runs and runs. He tries to find solace in several places, but Saul pursues him with men on horses, with dogs, and with his own spear. Finally, with no other place to go, he hides in the cave of Adullum.

Here's the great, anointed future king

   . . . the mighty warrior

      . . . the king's son-in-law

         . . . hiding for his life in a cave.

It would be easy for David to think that perhaps he'd been off course in his life calling. David could've imagined that Samuel may have been wrong about the anointing. The discouragement could have led him to believe he was headed in the wrong direction.

But he wasn't.

And perhaps you are not either.

Being Chased into a Cave

There is *one* common denominator for cave dwellers. It's what separates them from fish clingers. It is not our own actions and movements that force us into a cave. Someone or something always chases us there. We'd never go there without pursuers! David wouldn't have gone into the cave if it hadn't been for Saul's insane pursuit.

Sometimes our pursuers are people: a husband who demands that you work to make ends meet when your heart beats to be a stay-at-home mom; a boss who discourages you from moving forward every time you take him new ideas; some church "friends" who don't forgive or fail to restore long after you've repented and healed; a church leader who stands in the way of a new ministry that's just bursting from inside of you; a mother who wants you to wear a mask rather than talk about the abuse you knew as a child. Have you been chased into a cave by a person?

There is *one* common denominator for cave dwellers. It is not our own actions and movements that force us into a cave. Someone or something always chases us there.

Sometimes that which chases us into a cave is a painful event. A divorce you did not want. A car accident. Cancer. God's call to make big life changes to get out of debt. Even God's call to change the direction of your life to find His purpose can feel discouraging as you wait in a cave between the place you once were and the place where God is leading. Have you been chased into a cave by events or circumstances?

Whether it's a person or an event, it'll hurt. You'll be lonely.

My Cave

Several years ago, I was "at the top of my game," as they say. God had been blessing my work with teenage girls incredibly. I'd begun sharing my faith and leading teens and college-aged women to Christ. I was reaching the status of "best-selling" author. I was speaking at sold-out events. It seemed I had found my true purpose, and God was blessing it in every way.

Then came my cave.

One day I was listening to the voice of Pastor Erlo Stegen as it came across the Internet from Africa. He'd become a pastor to me personally, though he was an ocean away. His deep Bible teaching had led hundreds of thousands to Christ and to miraculous healing and deliverance from the hellish demonic forces that often thrive on the Dark Continent. His teaching breathed fresh life into me each time I tuned in.

"Can a mother forget the baby at her breast and have no compassion on the child she has borne? Though she may forget, I will never forget you . . ." Erlo read fervently.

What was that? I thought. I recognized a knowing coming across me as if I was being called to attention, pointed to, sought out. It was only a feeling, but so powerful. It was not emotion. It was a spiritual awareness.

I listened as Erlo explained the verse. ". . . but God does not forget *you*," he spoke as if directly to me.

I didn't like what I was getting. It was as if God were telling me that I was soon to be forgotten. By whom? Why?

I brushed it off, turning the Internet connection off and opening my Bible study. Halfway through, the terrible knowing returned as the author encouraged me to "Read Isaiah 49:14–16." Wouldn't you know it? Smack in the middle of that passage were the now-familiar words: "Can a mother forget the baby at her breast and have no compassion on the child she has borne? Though she may forget, I will not forget you!"

I had a knowing that something very bad was about to happen in my life. And it did. That very day, all hell broke loose.

I feel led to leave it at that, but oh, please don't let my lack of words project a lack of torment. The day seemed like a month. The darkness and oppression were thick. Spoken words cut deeply. I'm not ashamed to use the word *hell*, because what came out against me was from that place of darkness.

At 10:00 that night I picked up my pen again with much less faith in my heart to write:

Alone.

Oh God, the promises I claimed hours ago seem worlds away. I am afraid.

Yes, I know You will not forget me, but mothers are forgetting their babies, and the Church no longer loves its sinners. My heart aches with loneliness tonight.

The pain ran deep. It would be days until I ate. Weeks until I smiled. Months until I stopped crying every single day. Two years until I felt the Lord calling me out of the cave. I was lonely and questioned the very core of my calling.

Been there? Are you there now?

A Tale of Three Kings

Gene Edwards's *A Tale of Three Kings* portrays the period of David's life when he had to hide in Adullum. It's one of the most precious books I've ever read, and it enabled me to endure a deep period of discouragement that was, in fact, part of God's call on my life. Here's what Edwards writes about the caves of our lives:

> Caves are not the ideal place for morale building.
>
> David had less now than when he was a shepherd, for now he had no lyre, no sun, not even the company of the sheep. The memories of the court had faded. David's greatest ambition now reached no higher than a shepherd's staff. Everything was being crushed out of him.
>
> He sang a great deal.
>
> And matched each note with a tear.
>
> How strange, is it not, what suffering begets?
>
> There in those caves, drowned in the sorrow of his song and in the song of his sorrows, David became the greatest hymn writer and the greatest comforter of broken hearts this world shall ever know.[1]

"A man after God's own heart." That's what God called David. That was David's purpose in life. We think it was for him to be a king. That's what we see with our physical eyes. It's the title we think of quickly because we're so trained by this world's paradigms. We have to look with the eyes of our hearts to see David's truest purpose.

It was to sing songs.

To mingle bravery with tears of brokenness.

To show us how to feel, how to pray, how to hope, how to hurt, how to praise.

A man after God's own heart. This title has lived long beyond his crown as an earthly king. This was God's design for David.

Hiding for his life in a cave, David found the freedom to pursue it.

If you are in a cave, you must stay there. Don't poise yourself for action, and certainly don't fight your way out. Not now. Not yet.

Be still. Know that He is God . . . and that He will not for one moment forget you.

Making
It Work

Can a mother forget the baby at her breast and have no compassion on the child she has borne? Though she may forget, I will not forget you!

—Isaiah 49:15

Feeling forgotten by a figurative mother in your life? Or perhaps you've been driven into a cave by a horrible circumstance that others around you can't truly understand. What pain accompanies being driven into a cave! Feeling forgotten? God promises He will not forget you. Journal what the Lord speaks to you about this issue of being forgotten.

11

Being Still in Your Cave

Clang! Bam! Crunch!

The sliding closet door had fallen off the track . . . again. It had landed on my toe, and I'd felt the temptation to use a few extremely expressive words.

"*Ahhhhhhhh!*" *I screamed.*

Three months, *I said in my heart.* God, I told You I could live in this place for three months. It's been almost three years! I don't want to be here anymore.

Tears of frustration slipped down my cheeks.

I'm obeying You, God. Bob's obeying You, *I silently prayed from the floor.* When is it going to start paying off?

Since we'd moved, Bob sold our radio stations. But during the course of FCC approval, the new owners had significantly decreased our sales in a pointed and underhanded manner. That allowed them to purchase the stations for a price that was much lower than the one to which they had originally agreed.

What was supposed to be the first few years of blessing seemed to be filled with only sacrifice and tears. This wasn't how it was supposed to be.

Was it?

Does your discouragement come from being in a cave? It's not your own actions and sin that have pushed you here but those of someone else or circumstances beyond your control. Like me, you may think this isn't the way it is supposed to be. God may have a different view. This may be *exactly* how it is supposed to be. So, what do you do while you're in a cave?

Be still!

Oh, this doesn't mean you aren't taking action. It's just the kind of action that no one will ever see. When you're in a cave, you've got to recognize who drove you there, and you've got to know how to respond.

Who Drove You Here?

At first glance, it would seem that Saul drove David into his cave. It's certainly a good sign that you're in a cave when you can identify a person or an event, but is that person or event who or what really drove you to this place? No. You see, Saul had a little help from an invisible friend.

First Samuel 18:10–11 says that "an evil spirit from God came forcefully upon Saul. He was prophesying in his house, while David was playing the harp, as he usually did. Saul had a spear in his hand and he hurled it, saying to himself, 'I'll pin David to the wall.' But David eluded him twice."

The book of Ephesians warns us that when we are in the battle of freedom, we're not going to be fighting against the people and things of this world. Our battle, says the apostle Paul, is not against flesh and blood. It is really against the forces of darkness in this world. It's against Satan and his minions.

Your enemy is not the person who has driven you into this cave. It's not your boss. Not your husband. Not your mom. Not the person you once thought was a friend. It's not an event either. Who drove you here? Satan. If you fail to recognize Satan as your enemy, you may be tempted to take action and fight against the quiet waiting that God requires in this place of discouragement.

It's really important to know that Satan did not drive you here without God's permission. Certainly poor old Job spent some time in a cave. He lost his wealth, his family, and his health in a matter of days. Before Satan was allowed to touch him, he had to get permission from God. Job 1:6–12 unfolds a conversation between God and Satan from which Bible scholars conclude two important things. First, those actively in the center of God's will are targets for Satan's attacks. Second, Satan cannot attack you without permission from God.

> If you fail to recognize Satan as your enemy, you may be tempted to take action and fight against the quiet waiting that God requires in this place of discouragement.

Who has driven you into this cave? You must recognize that Satan has done this *with God's permission.*

How Do You Respond to God?

When stuck in a cave, the temptation is to respond to people by rising up in disagreement, rebellion, or even gossip. Or sometimes we become overly focused on Satan, rebuking him at every turn and crying, "spiritual warfare." I think those actions would be a mistake. It is God's will for you to be in a cave if you are in one. It is His will that you submit to it.

It was God's will for David to be chased into that cave by

Give Thanks

*Always giving
thanks to God
the Father for
everything, in the
name of our Lord
Jesus Christ. Submit
to one another out of
reverence for Christ.*

—Ephesians 5:20–21

Saul, who was really controlled by an evil spirit. If anyone in history could have defended himself, David could have. Remember, the people were chanting, "Saul has killed his thousands. But David his tens of thousands" (1 Sam. 18:7, author's paraphrase). David would have won the popular vote. He didn't seek it. He sought God's purpose. He quieted his heart.

This is the perfect time to head back to our treasure chest of purpose—the Bible—for a big, golden nugget of truth. Ephesians 5:20–21 says that we are to be "always giving thanks to God the Father for everything, in the name of our Lord Jesus Christ. Submit to one another out of reverence for Christ." God doesn't just call you to give thanks to Him when hitting the mark of His purpose is an easy road of blissful moments. He calls us to give thanks in *everything*! Even in our caves.

I had a reminder of our call to give thanks this past summer. My husband was in a life-threatening Jet-Ski accident. (Go ahead. Laugh! We do. The words *life-threatening* and *Jet Ski* just don't seem to work together, do they?) But this was a cave, to be sure. Bob and I were again really enjoying the blessings of serving God when, suddenly, we found ourselves in a cave created by life events.

I will never forget that brief moment in my kitchen when, for a split second, I wondered if my husband would walk again as I took what I refer to as *the phone call*. The doctor explained that Bob's pelvis had been broken in two places and that only the skin held one of his legs in place. He explained the critical nature of the injury and that many patients bleed out and die when the sharp pelvic bones sever arteries.

I still remember the sound of the mother screaming for her baby's life as I waited hours later in the trauma ER for a word on Bob's condition. I remember the eight-hour surgery two days later and crying when the anesthesiologist came out with gentle words but no assurances. I remember the painkillers, the long nights, and the longer days we endured in that first month of recovery. (No small challenge for a wife who's not a very natural nurturer.) And just when I was about to think we could make it through this cave, we got another phone call.

"You may have to start over," the doctor said, explaining that Bob's repaired pelvic bones had shifted. "We need more X-rays, and if the shift is more than two centimeters, we'll have to do surgery again. This one will be longer and more intense than the first."

Longer? More intense? How was that possible?

"We can't start over, God," I cried as I crawled onto the sofa. "Please! What is Your plan in this? Will You show me?"

I began to channel surf and came upon Joyce Meyers.

"Always give thanks to God the Father in everything . . ."

"In all you do, give thanks . . ."

"And give thanks, whatever happens."

I began to journal all the things God had gifted to me in this time of healing.

I thank You, God. This burden is easy.
I thank You, God. Our friends are faithful.
I thank You, God. We have a great staff.
I thank You, God. My brother comes to visit us with Rebecca
    each day.
I thank You, God. Lexi has a school to attend.

111

I thank You, God. It is quiet and rainy today.
I thank You, God. Bobby and I love each other.
I thank You, God. Robby loves You.

Each of these was a blessing I was able to see *only* through my time in the cave. As I sat there, peace began to cover me. I changed from worrier to worshipper. It was enough. Just thanking God there in my cave was all I needed to do.

> First and foremost, when you're in a cave, you've got to respond to God with thanksgiving.

The phone interrupted the silence. It was the doctor. "Hello," I answered hopefully.

"Mrs. Gresh, I have good news for you," came the doctor's kind voice. Bob was not going to have to start over.

I'm not saying you'll always get your way. But giving thanks to God is the key in the cave. I've been in caves before when I got not one material thing I pleaded for. But I still got the peace. God always brings us peace when we praise and thank Him.

First and foremost, when you're in a cave, you've got to respond to God with thanksgiving.

But, Really, How Do You Respond to Others?

Well, closely linked to God's call to give thanks is Ephesians 5:21, which says, "Submit to one another out of reverence for

Christ." Seems to me that when we most want to take someone out, we ought to submit instead.

> " It has been said that it is impossible to forgive a man who deliberately hurts you for the sole purpose of destroying you or lowering you. If this be true, you have but one hope: to see this unfair hurt as coming by permission from God for the purpose of lifting your stature above that place where formerly you stood.[1]
>
> —Gene Edwards, *The Prisoner in the Third Cell* "

God tells you and me to give thanks to Him and submit to each other. (Sounds like "Be still" to me.) I remember several years ago having a pastor rise up against me. I was scheduled to speak to his youth group, and though he didn't have a problem with me, he had a problem with someone closely connected to me. He told the youth pastor to tell a youth worker to tell me it might be best if I didn't keep the engagement. (He chased me into a tiny little cave!) I quickly processed the whole thing through tear-filled eyes.

"You are allowing Satan to use this pastor to discourage me. How do I respond?" I prayed.

My flesh wanted to make some phone calls. First, to the pastor to tell him he was a coward for not calling me himself. Second, to the youth pastor to see if he was willing to support this lunacy. Third, to the elders of the church to report the pastor. But I heard God whispering, *Be still, Dannah. Give thanks. Submit.*

I drew a bubble bath and hopped inside. (Where else is a girl to cry her eyes out?) I praised God in that steamy haven of my cave. I submitted to the pastor's foolishness only because it demonstrated that I trusted my God to work it all out.

He did.

The next day the youth pastor called me. He told me his authority was the elder board, and one of them just happened to hear about the pastor's paranoia. Apparently, the elders confronted the issue. They had no problem with my teaching at their church and asked would I please consider still coming.

The Lord is my defender. How beautiful it is to see Him rise up to defend me when I obey His Word by giving Him thanks and submitting to others out of reverence for Christ.

In the cave it is time to be still! No alliances. No retaliation. No well-thought plans. Don't even try to figure out why you are there. Most often the caves in our lives don't make sense for a long, long time. Just be still. Give God thanks. Submit to others out of reverence to God. The sooner you rest and accept it, the sooner you'll find God leading you toward that sunshine at the cave's mouth. The sooner you'll sense His precious voice calling. When you hear that, it's time to move!

So how do you know if you are hearing God's calling? How do you know if you've been still in your cave long enough? Or if it's time to let go of that fish because you know where you're headed? Well, I have five questions that will help you know. Answering these will point you to the life that God designed for you. Join me in the next part of this book as we use fun, practical tools to identify the call in your life.

Making It Work

Always giving thanks to God the Father for everything, in the name of our Lord Jesus Christ. Submit to one another out of reverence for Christ.

—Ephesians 5:20–21

Having been introduced to the concept of both holding on to fish and being in a cave, journal about your own current situation? Is God calling you to make some changes by letting go of some fish, or is He calling you to be still in your cave? The answer to this is very critical to how you will approach the five little questions that reveal the life God designed for you.

PART THREE

FIVE LITTLE QUESTIONS THAT REVEAL THE LIFE GOD DESIGNED FOR YOU

"You were made by God and for God, and until you understand that, life will never make sense. Only in God do we discover our origin, our identity, our meaning, our purpose, our significance and our destiny."

—Rick Warren

12

Do I Need a Fresh Infusion of Grace?

A crumbling seat made of a concrete step. A crack in the sidewalk below my feet. The scent of pine. A tiny American flag staked into the grass nearby.

These are my memories. A picture in my mind that is long staying.

It happened when I was only four and a half. A simple neighborhood Bible club awakened my heart to the love of Jesus and my own sin. I didn't understand much more than that. I honestly wonder what kind of sin I could have brought to Jesus to confess that day. Did I steal a toy from my little brother? Stomp my feet at my mother? I don't know. But I know there was an awareness of my separation from God. And the promise of a lifelong love affair with Jesus Christ.

My Savior.

Welcome to the *five little questions*! I believe that answering these questions will reveal the life that God designed just for you. The questions will confirm that you're already there, giving you a boost of much-needed encouragement, or they will reveal where you are very off course. Either result is important, giving you confidence to move forward into your calling.

Let's begin. Let me ask you, "Do you need a fresh infusion of grace?"

Amazing Grace

John Newton didn't care much for God. Not until March 1748, anyway.

That's when he almost died on a ship carrying gold, ivory, and beeswax across the high seas. In the midst of a tumultuous storm, he found himself pleading with God for forgiveness from his seedy and blasphemous life. The ship finally drifted to Ireland where Newton spent six weeks devouring the Word of God. He seemed a changed man.

He was hired to work on another ship headed to Africa. Upon arrival, he relapsed into sexual sin and cruelly shackled his new load of cargo—slaves—into the pit of the ship. While he mourned his sexual sin and repented, he did not even see his sin as a slave trader. He did not see that tying humans in the depths of a boat on top of one another, where many would die, was murderous. That each time he sold a young, beautiful African girl into sexual slavery, he was an accomplice to the atrocities she would experience. He was blind to the fact that branding these free men and women to lives of torturous labor was completely contrary to God's will. He did not *see* his sin. You see, slave trading was common. It was the norm of the day. Many owned slaves, Christians and non-Christians alike. Newton was just blending in with the crowd. After ten years, a seizure required Newton to change his career. He retired from the slave-trading "business."

Years passed. (Oh, how I love that little sentence. It reminds me of God's long-suffering.) Finally, Newton saw his sin. You and I can only imagine the tears he shed in repentance. We can only guess that he went through a period of questioning if God could ever use him. Ah, but He did. John Newton became a key voice in the abolition of slavery. Recall with me these words that he wrote during this new season of his life:

> *Amazing grace*
> *How sweet the sound*
> *That saved a wretch like me*
> *I once was lost, but now am found*
> *Was blind, but now I see.*

Yes, Newton penned the famous hymn "Amazing Grace"—not the first time he surrendered or the second, but the third time he finally got the concept of grace. If anyone ever needed grace, he did. If anyone was ever off course from the purpose of his life, he was. His life was scandalous! Sex and slavery! For years he thought it was his purpose. It wasn't. It was a nasty, slimy fish—an ensnarement. If God can get John Newton on track to live a God-designed life, certainly He can do it for you and me too!

The Anthem of the New Testament

Grace is the anthem of the New Testament, but we'll look at just one book, Ephesians. Why? It's the apostle Paul's treatise on purpose! Eight times in the first three chapters of Ephesians Paul mentions the source of a God-designed life. It is grace. Look with me at a few of the verses. Don't just skim over these, friend. The most powerful words in this book are ones you may have read again and again in your own Bible. Savor these verses with me (words are italicized for emphasis).

Grace and peace to you from God our Father
and the Lord Jesus Christ.
—Ephesians 1:2

Because of his love, God had already decided
to make us his own children through Jesus Christ. That
was what he wanted and what pleased him, and *it brings
praise to God because of his wonderful grace. God gave that
grace freely*, in Christ, the One he loves.
—Ephesians 1:5–6 NCV

How rich is God's grace, which he
has given to us so fully and freely.
—Ephesians 1:7–8 NCV

It is by *grace* you have been saved.
—Ephesians 2:5

And he raised us up with Christ and gave us a seat with him
in the heavens. He did this for those in Christ Jesus *so that for
all future time he could show the very great riches of his grace.*
—Ephesians 2:6–7 NCV

For it is *by grace you have been saved*, through faith—
and this not from yourselves, it is the gift of God.
—Ephesians 2:8

Surely you have heard about the administration of
God's grace that was given to me for you.
—Ephesians 3:2

By *God's special gift of grace* given to me through his
power, I became a servant to tell that Good News.
—Ephesians 3:7 NCV

It is only by God's special gift of grace that you will ever be free to pursue your purpose. With all our high-priced corporate ladder training and user-friendly books on talents, personality types, and gifts, we often begin the pursuit of our life purpose with . . . well, *us!*

What do I like? How do I work? Where should I train? We begin with *us.* Nothing could put us further off course.

If your life purpose is not God-designed, you'll just end up discouraged, confused, and unfulfilled. And so many Christians are living these depleted lives of mediocrity because they've never slowed down to ask God how he designed them to live. I once was one of them until I learned that finding my purpose began with God. More specifically, it begins with His grace. Grasp that!

The Ring of Grace

GOD'S BEST

the Ring of Grace

Back to that mark . . . that specific and preplanned design of your life. It's been a few chapters since we talked about it. Recall with me that the God-designed purpose of your life is found when you live in the dead center of the bull's-eye. Anything less than hitting God's purpose for your life in every area—purity, joyfulness, financial stewardship, and even your vocational platform for your purpose—is sin. *Chatta.* That's right. Failing to find your life's purpose is sin. Let's look more closely at the word in the next few chapters.

There are three distinct parts of the mark or bull's-eye. Each represents a vital part of our purpose. I believe that you cannot even begin to live in the riches of God's purpose for your life until you first make a willful choice to accept Christ's gift of grace. In doing so, you build a *ring of grace* around your life. How do you do this? Surrender. In humility surrender your unbelievable neediness to Christ's forgiveness.

We often make the mistake of believing that the ring of grace is something we enter just once and the work is all done. I don't think that's entirely accurate. Though there really does have to be a willful moment of decision, like the one I described at the beginning of this chapter, we don't stay in that ring of grace very well if we leave it at that.

In Revelation 3:20 Christ says, "Here I am! I stand at the door and knock. If you hear my voice and open the door, I will come in and eat with you, and you will eat with me" (NCV). We often use this passage to talk to those who've never surrendered their lives to Jesus, but that would be a big mistake. This verse is for you. It is for me. This passage of Revelation was written to the *church* of Laodicea. Believers. God doesn't address non-issues in the Bible. I think He writes this verse to remind us that we need to be constantly resurrendering our lives to Christ. Perhaps some of us need a fresh infusion of grace.

A Fresh Infusion of Grace

John Newton first surrendered his life to Christ when he was almost shipwrecked.

But he didn't stay in that ring of grace. I'm not suggesting that he lost his salvation. But his life lost the benefits, the rewards of hitting the dead center of the mark.

I can identify. I slipped. As a Christian teenager who loved Jesus Christ dearly, I slipped. I never willfully walked away from the mark, but slowly, one thing after another intoxicated me.

I came to a point in my life where I needed a fresh infusion of grace. "Here I am!" Christ called to me. "I stand at the door and knock. If you hear my voice and open the door, I will come in and eat with you, and you will eat with me."

It was as if I'd never even known my Savior before. Please understand, I'm not suggesting I lost what I received when I was four and a half. I don't believe that for a second. I just needed more of it. Not because Christ hadn't done it well the first time, but my spirit had forgotten. My fresh infusion of grace went something like this:

A warm leather driver's seat in my brand new Dodge Caravan.

A crack in my life that no one knew about.

The scent of my new baby girl coming up from the backseat.

A grimy four-lane highway nearby.

These are my memories. A picture in my mind that is long-staying.

When I was twenty-six, a simple Christian radio program reawakened my heart to the love of Jesus and the enormous reality of my sinfulness. I was finally beginning to understand. I didn't have to wonder what kind of sin I had to bring to Jesus to confess that day. I had given the gift of my innocence away. I was worshipping the idols of success and money. I was missing my children's most precious years consumed by workaholism. I knew. Though I'd never stopped loving Him or being loved, Jesus was not Lord of my life. I was bearing the scars of separation from God in all my picture-perfect Christianity. I wanted to come back to the promise of a lifelong love affair with Jesus Christ.

My Savior.

Covenant Power

I am absolutely in love with God's covenant. It is the core of our faith. I've written about it in nearly all of my books, so I won't rehash things here. But if you've never understood covenant, I recommend that you read Our Covenant God *by Kay Arthur or* Lost Secrets of the Covenant *by Malcolm Smith.*

Many around me saw the enormous change in my life. My husband and mother saw it and cheered me on. I was more at peace, less into perfection. I was more playful, less into workaholism. I was more full of joy, less living in stress. I was diving into the mark for the first time in my adult life.

And I loved it.

Do you need a fresh infusion of grace? There's a wealth of it just waiting for you. It is and has always been the instruction of God to continually dip into His reservoir of grace. I believe that, had I practiced dipping into that place of grace, I'd have never slipped so far away.

Old Testament Recovenanting

During Old Testament times, God's people were called to practice animal sacrifice as a form of dipping again and again into God's grace. This was what they called covenanting and recovenanting with God. I won't go deeply into covenant here, but suffice it to say that it requires us to hit the bull's-eye and rewards us with amazing blessings that will blow us away. To hit the bull's-eye in Old Testament days, you had to start with animal sacrifice. There had to be blood.

To be sure, it was a gory and horrific ritual meant to reflect the gore and horror of separation from God. A Hebrew word that described this act was *beryth*, which meant to separate. In separating the lamb and walking between the bloody parts, the Israelites

126

remembered how good God had been in protecting them, providing for them, and staying near to them although their sin made them worthy only of separation.

The Israelite priests sacrificed two lambs every day as a general atonement for the sins of all of Israel. In addition, anyone who'd committed certain specific sins brought a private offering to God. Many lambs died as the Israelites recovenanted with God— as they dipped again and again into the covenant to be infused with God's forgiveness. In fact, the annual Passover feast invited Jewish families to *each* sacrifice a lamb to recovenant. On one Passover day, it was recorded that the priests sacrificed 256,500 lambs on behalf of the Jewish people in the city of Jerusalem alone![1] Following the Passover sacrifice, each family went home to eat of the lamb they had sacrificed. They recognized that to be fully recovenanted with God, they had to *eat the lamb*.

New Testament Recovenanting

God makes the covenant far less gory for us as New Testament believers. He Himself was the Lamb whose blood was shed. We need simply to accept this act of grace to enter into the ring of grace. Sadly, many New Testament believers take this grace one time and do not recovenant, even though when Jesus introduced communion, He asked us to do it *often* in remembrance of our covenant. He was establishing a way for you and me to recovenant with God regularly—to receive a fresh infusion of grace. To early New Testament believers who were not so far from the Old Testament sacrifices, this was a private act. Only believers were permitted to attend. This secrecy often resulted in insane gossip that the early believers were committing acts of human sacrifice or that they were cannibals. This did not deter them, for they understood that to be in the family of God meant to eat the lamb

127

as their ancestors had been doing since the first Passover. They remembered their original covenant each time they took of the wine and the bread, figuratively eating the Lamb of God.

The communion rituals of some believers today are poor representations of that holy, private recovenanting. Many have reduced the great meal and the holy passing of the cup and bread to some fast-food type of tradition that gets tacked onto the end of an occasional worship service. A tiny plastic cup of grape juice and an economical square of a cracker are quickly passed and unemotionally taken. Shame on us! No wonder we are so often in need of a fresh infusion of grace. We may not get it regularly as we should with the shallow ritual that communion has become in some places of worship. (Don't be offended if this is not the case in your congregation, but if you are offended, take it to God. Ask Him if it is true, and what you should do about it.)

> Many have reduced the great meal and the holy passing of the cup and bread to some fast-food type of tradition that gets tacked onto the end of an occasional worship service.

Last weekend, I decided to do something about it. In Griffin, Georgia, we taught a few hundred teenagers about eating the lamb, and we took a full hour to take communion. No little cups. No little crackers. We had large goblets of *the blood* and loaves of flat bread for *the body*. After about thirty minutes of repentance to consider how we may have broken the covenant since the last time we'd partaken, we approached one of the pastors to eat of the Lamb of God.

As I approached Pastor Sam, I was wholly undone by the

unworthiness of my sin. I began to fear I might lose composure. Certainly this was not the experience I was used to having with communion. The worship. The confession. The contemplation of the Lamb was culminating into a far different experience for me. Sam looked me right in the eyes and said, "Dannah, this is the blood and body of Christ. It was sacrificed for you." That was it. I *was* undone. I moved to the kneeling bench and wept. The pain of my sin was very real at that moment.

The holiness of the sacrament was not wasted that day. I watched junior-high boys barely make it back to their seats before they let the tears flow. How often do you see a young man that age connect so deeply with his Savior? I watched college-aged girls drop to their knees or fall against the wall as if it was holding them up. The Spirit recovenanted with us in such a way that we knew He was very real. There was such holiness at the table of remembrance that day.

This is the greatest barrier to sin. This is what keeps us in the ring of grace. This is what sets us free from the snares in our lives.

I wonder . . .

If we took the time to properly recovenant with God as we're called to, would as many of us venture so far out of the ring of grace as I once did? As perhaps you have? Would we be less likely to need a complete fresh infusion of God's grace if we simply took time to truly embrace the heart of Christ's invitation?

"This do in remembrance of Me."

Maybe, like me, you've found yourself living in a self-designed life. One that's a horrible reflection of God. It didn't happen willfully, but slowly you have slipped into studying for a career that the world deems worthy. Or worshipping your children more than you worship God. Or investing your life into the décor of your home rather than the mission field around you. Or pursuing secret sins rather than God's grace.

> Would we be less likely to need a complete fresh infusion of God's grace if we simply took time to truly embrace the heart of Christ's invitation?
>
> "This do in remembrance of Me."

Need a fresh infusion of grace? Don't wait. Receive it today. Right where you are, ask the Lord to once again become the Lord of your life. He's never stopped being your Savior, but His tender mark of satisfaction has long since been taken as He seeks to make you hungry for the life He designed for you. Reach out for it now. Not by passing yet another final exam. Not by assisting your children in earning yet another award. Not by buying your way into the home-of-the-year parlor tour. It's certainly not in that secret sin. Reach out for it on your knees.

You need look no further for the beginning of the trail for the life God designed for you. This is it.

Making It Work

Here I am! I stand at the door and knock. If you hear my voice and open the door, I will come in and eat with you, and you will eat with me.

—Revelation 3:20 NCV

At this point, the *Five Little Questions That Reveal the Life God Designed for You* study guide becomes invaluable. I'll still offer you a brief journaling assignment here, but the study guide actually helps you to create a life M.A.P. (My Action Plan) that guides you to the life God designed for you. If you are still opting to stick with journaling, today I'd like you to examine your heart to see if you need a fresh infusion of grace. Write about it.

13

Am I Working in Agreement with My Created Personality?

"You have almost no extroversion in you, Dannah." I remembered back to the day I'd first heard those words many years ago. Bob and I had hired a professional development consultation to take key personnel through the Highlands Program, a comprehensive two-day personality skills and inventory testing.

"You're an extreme introvert," voiced the consultant, showing me my evaluation.

"But I like to be with people," I countered.

"That's a common misunderstanding," she answered. "Just because you're an introvert doesn't mean you don't like people. It means that you are most likely to be energized by alone time and in work environments that allow you to be independent and quiet. A work environment that forces you to be with people all day will drain you very quickly. Extroverts tend to be energized by people and drained if they have too much alone time."

That day, God pulled the handle on an entire energy facility for me. Figuring out who I was gave me permission to do what I was called to do.

My children are God's proof that each of us is uniquely different. Lexi is an extreme extrovert with artistic, creative skills that cause me to marvel. She likes to be touching someone if at all possible. My friend calls her a Velcro-child. Maybe you have one. Robby is a balanced introvert with math skills that make me feel a tad on the stupid side. He likes his space. If I am not careful, I could place undue expectations on them that frustrate their unique differences.

Proverbs 22:6 encourages us to "Train a child in the way he should go." It is heavy-laden with treasure for us whether we are mothers or not. The first word, *train*, is *chanak*, an archer's term like the word for sin, *chatta*. This word was used specifically to describe a soldier training with his bow. The bows these ancient Hebrew marksmen trained with were not the gadgety high-tech kind you and I see these days. Known as compound bows, modern bows can be adjusted to allow hunters of different sizes, strength, and skill to use them easily.

This was not so with the ancient longbow. The bows these marksmen used were one simple piece of slightly curving wood. Each bow was uniquely different. Therefore, the hunter would need to adjust *himself* to the bow. He'd need to learn the bow's unique strengths and characteristics.

It gets even better. We're told to "train [*chanak*] a child in the way he should go." The Hebrew word for "the way he should go" is *derek,* which literally means *according to the bent.* It refers to the unique inner design or direction of the child. The phrase "the way he should go" doesn't speak of some prescribed path that every man, woman, and child should take. It's not talking about rules to live by. Rather, it is referring to a specific path that's just for this child. His or her unique design.

I'm fairly certain that if my Robby were a longbow, he'd be made of a solid, beautiful wood. Perhaps maple hardwood. He'd be strong. Steady. Focused. Unassuming.

Lexi? Well, she'd be made of curly willow! Unpredictable. Untamed. Whimsical. Light-hearted.

Somehow, I've got to know each of them so intimately that I'm able to help them direct the arrows of their lives directly at the mark God has created just for them. Not yours. Not mine. Theirs.

> The phrase "the way he should go" doesn't speak of some prescribed path that every man, woman, and child should take. It's not talking about rules to live by.

Now, if you are a mom, I hope you're getting a boost of encouragement from this, but there is a life lesson in this for all of us—moms or not. Think of yourself as the child. Like Robby or Lexi, you and I are created with unique bents. The amount of time we need alone is probably not the same. Our ability to focus will vary. Some like details, and others hate them. Some take risks and make new things happen. Others create the steady safety of routine. We are all uniquely different. Are you working in agreement with your created personality?

Designed to Be Fulfilled

In the last chapter, I mentioned that you'd never find your God-designed life by starting with yourself. Never. But I do believe that once you are walking consistently in God's ring of grace, it's time to examine who He created you to be. Ever find yourself utterly frustrated with your life's work, holding on to the fish of performance or a title or a paycheck, then finding that it doesn't seem to be worth it? Or maybe you're a stay-at-home mom who keeps volunteering for things that only seem to drain you. Or perhaps you're a stay-at-home mom who desperately needs an outlet to be with other people. Perhaps you are a student majoring in nursing because you love people, but you've found that the details overwhelm you. I realize that some of the things in our lives must be done out of maturity. But many times our discouragement arises when we work against our personality strengths. When we do, our life's work isn't fulfilling.

Dr. Charles F. Boyd sums up the dilemma we all face when he writes: "When God made you, he put in your heart strengths, capabilities, potential skills, passions, drives and motivations. He designed you with a certain way of being. As a result, you feel fulfilled when you are acting according to your design—and frustrated when you don't."[1]

Yes, we're finally getting to the practical part of living in freedom to pursue God's design for your life. You see, your mark is different from mine. You're created with a specific call on your life, and it has everything to do with how you are uniquely different.

Adornment of Charis

GOD'S BEST

the Ring of Grace

The Adornment of Charis

Getting into the ring of grace is just the first part of hitting the mark. Another vital part is what I call *the adornment of charis. Charis* is the Greek word for grace. It literally means *gift.* It also means *favor, benefit,* and *blessing.* A very significant part of God's grace is discovering the unique way He's going to favor your life with a gift to demonstrate His power. This is His adornment of charis. It's the part of you that's not like anyone else. Your unique bent if you will. It's the specific way God designed you to be fulfilled.

If you are feeling frustrated with where you are in your station in life, it could be because you are working outside of your special personality strengths and capabilities. This is a great time to pull out any old personality inventories you have taken such as the DiSC or the Myers-Briggs inventory. If you've never taken one, there is one in my study guide for this book. I highly recommend you take it before proceeding.

Since the Marston inventory, commonly known as the DiSC inventory, is public domain, and I can get you somewhat pegged without actually taking the test, we're going to look toward it in answering question number two of our five little questions.

There are two basic measurements for this inventory: people-interaction preference and pace preference. So first consider whether you are fueled up and most animated by being with people and find yourself becoming quietly drained when faced with large segments of time alone. Or are you fueled up by alone time and find that you have to rest after

Personality Profiling

There are various instruments to profile the personality and/or psychological structure of a person. The following have been around for a while and are highly credible.

DiSC

The DiSC test is widely used because it is public domain. Developed as the Marston Behavior test by a psychologist, it is short and easy to score.[2] You may have taken a version of this behavior preference profile. A version of it is available in my study guide for this book. There are many versions of it available online.

Myers-Briggs

The Myers & Briggs Foundation developed a more in-depth inventory of personality and psychological profiling. You can learn more about how and where you can take the inventory at www.myersbriggs.org.

The Highlands Ability Battery (www.highlandsco.com)

This inventory is the most intense of the different versions. It tests everything from behavioral preferences to memory to musical skills such as pitch and rhythm. It is very expensive and time-consuming, but God used it to change my life almost ten years ago.

being drained by excessive time with people? Which are you?

Extroverted	*or*	Introverted
Energized by people		*Energized by alone time*

Now consider the pace at which you are most comfortable working? Do you prefer accomplishing multiple tasks at a fast pace in a single day and find yourself bored with details and routine? Or do you prefer to work more slowly and methodically on a single task in a day and find yourself frustrated with people who work quickly?

Fast-paced	*or*	Slow-paced
Multitasker		*Focused tasker*

When you put these two basic behavior preferences together, you have one of four core behavioral styles:

1. Introverted and fast-paced
2. Extroverted and fast-paced
3. Extroverted and slow-paced
4. Introverted and slow-paced

John Trent and Gary Smalley have come up with some tremendous portraits to help us remember our behavioral preferences and their character strengths.

They write about them in their children's book entitled *The Treasure Tree*.[3] They've given each personality a symbolic animal. I think this makes it so much easier to remember.

Whatever you are, note it on the chart by placing a star at the spot that best reflects where you are. For example, I'm introverted and fast-paced (Lion) with a strange tendency to slow down slightly for more details (Beaver). So my star would be placed on the line between Lion and Beaver to the far left since I don't have a lot of anything else in me.

Lions—introverted and fast-paced

If you are a true lion, you are aggressive, assertive, like to lead, and are very task oriented. You want to get the job done. You are a good decision maker, a direct leader, and always on the go with something new.

On the flip side, you might be a little impatient with people and tend not to be concerned with how they're feeling. You may be too controlling and might find details and routine work frustrating.

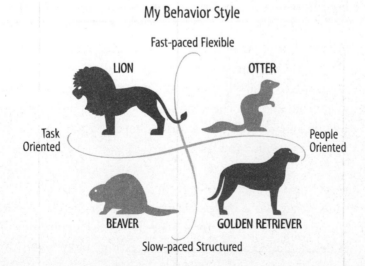

Otters—extroverted and fast-paced

Otters are the life of the party. If you are one, you are friendly and enthusiastic and extremely flexible. You are strongly interested in influencing people and motivating them. You're a strong opinion leader and like to invite everyone to the party.

Only problem is, you forget the details. So when we get to the party, there may not be any snacks. (My dear otter of a husband recently planned a Monday night football party at my house in central Pennsylvania. Everyone showed up. He and I were in California that night!) You may even forget the goal and be sidetracked by something else. You need to develop the discipline to follow through with tasks and avoid work environments where you are in charge of all the details.

Golden Retrievers—extroverted and slow-paced

If you think of yourself as a golden retriever, you're loyal, supportive, and loving. You're very interested in how everyone feels and are great at helping people understand one another. You bring unity to the table. You love a position that enables you to be cooperative and supportive. You are great nurturers. (My mom is a golden retriever and is the mom of all moms!)

You may find that you have a hard time being assertive when you really need to be, but with some discipline this will come. Don't place yourself in a work environment in which you have to confront and manage a lot. It will stress you out. You also don't like change and are uncomfortable with a work environment that doesn't offer stability.

Beavers—introverted and slow-paced

Finally, what about the beavers? You love to work. You are busy all the time, making sure all the details are taken care of. You are detailed and cautious, so you get things done well. You enjoy work environments where you can be somewhat independent and organized.

You just might need to be flexible from time to time to be a good part of the group. Sometimes you are considered inflexible or rigid. You don't like to be in an environment where the pace is fast and always changing.

Study yourself for a while and figure yourself out. (Remember, if you're struggling with this basic overview, there is an entire inventory in my study guide that will help.) Why is this important? Well, I found it to be the foundational building block to understanding my unique design—the parts of me that God created to be just me. Without this step, I'd still be wondering why I was so frustrated with my marketing job. As a Lion/Beaver, I'm very task oriented. I'm not people oriented, which makes me somewhat of an introvert. As a result, my marketing job, which kept me in client meetings, staff brainstorming sessions, and sales events, drained me. I needed solitude so I could get tasks done. When we realized this, Bob, who was also my boss, put me in charge of marketing research and analysis of marketing surveys. And he moved my office into our house, so I only came to the main office for necessary meetings. What a happy book-geek I was! This was a baby step closer to God's design for me.

So where do you think you might be? Do you need more alone time? more people time? a faster pace? a slower one? See a change you need to make? I encourage you to do something that doesn't completely modify your life just yet. Something simple like moving your office to your home might be a good idea. Was it somewhat mundane and ordinary for me to make that change? You bet. But I wasn't ready for more just yet. (Remember, baby steps.) Maybe you feel that the place you're in is mundane or ordinary at times. Rest assured, God is using that place to strengthen your special strengths and abilities while you figure out your purpose. Even if we don't "get it," He's on it. He's developing you.

Now for the most exciting part of the adornment of charis. Not only did God create you with specific personality strengths, but He also has gifted you with something that is not of this world. Let's take a look at your spiritual gifts in the next chapter.

Making It Work

Train a child in the way he should go, and when he is old he will not turn from it.

—Proverbs 22:6

Write a flow-of-consciousness entry that expresses whatever frustrations you may be facing in your current position in life. Talk to the Lord about what changes you may need to make to feel more confident.

14

What Is My Supernatural Ability?

Here in the cave of my rental house, I was learning to hear from God. Feasting on His presence. My leather chair was marked with the claw marks of my faithful cocker spaniel, as she always cuddled up beside me while I meditated on God's Word.

I wasn't quite prepared for what today brought.

I pulled out my journal to record it.

May 24, 2002

God affirmed the gift of prophecy in me today. Numbers 12:6: "When a prophet of the LORD is among you, I reveal myself to him in visions, I speak to him in dreams." This has been a long time in being revealed to me. Teach me more, Lord, as I do not understand.

I put the pen down.

"Prophet? Isn't that an Old Testament gift, God?" I prayed. "Or for sure one abused by an awful lot of men and women today? Do you mind if I say . . . well, I'm not entirely comfortable with what You've said to me today. I really need more."

When you first submitted to Jesus Christ and entered into His ring of grace, at that *very moment*, God gifted you with a specific supernatural ability that He wants you to use. Hebrews 2:3–4 says that one of the evidences of your salvation is a specific, Holy Spirit–appointed spiritual skill, which we often call spiritual gifts. The next big question you need to answer in your quest to discover God's design for you is "What is my supernatural ability?"

A supernatural ability is not necessarily a talent you had before you came to Christ, though there may have been an inkling of it there. It may be far beyond your normal abilities. For example, some have the gift of discernment. It's the ability to sense things that are happening in the spiritual realm though you have no physical evidence of it. A lot of times women who have it mistakenly call it mere *women's intuition*. You may have sensed it when you knew you needed to pray for someone's marriage even though it looked picture-perfect. Within a few months, you found out that they were separated. Or it may come as an awakening in the night with a strong urge to pray for someone though you don't know what she is doing. The next day you wake up to find that she was in a car accident that could have been life-threatening.

Do you see how this is a gift that a woman couldn't possibly have in her natural ability? It's a supernatural ability. That's what makes it a spiritual gift—you couldn't possibly have this skill without God.

Unwrapped Gifts

According to Barna Research Online, 71 percent of believers have heard of spiritual gifts. Only 31 percent of them can name one they believe they possess. Twenty-one percent don't believe they have one. That's up pretty drastically from 1995 when only 4 percent didn't feel they had a spiritual gift.[1]

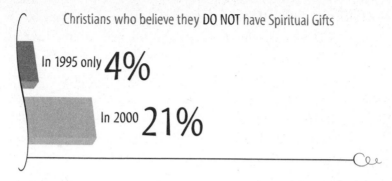

Christians who believe they **DO NOT** have Spiritual Gifts

In 1995 only **4%**

In 2000 **21%**

Look at Ephesians 4:7–8: "But to *each one of us* grace has been given as Christ . . . gave gifts to men" (italics added). *Each one of us* has received a gift. (And might I just note that its source is grace!) Some of us don't even know we have a spiritual gift. We walk around whining about how talented everyone else is. (Come on, we're being real with each other here. You've never been jealous of someone else's ability to serve God? I sure have!) All the while, a gift is just hovering in front of us, waiting to be opened!

Worse yet, you find yourself dreading your Sunday service of nursery duty and wonder why. Maybe there's a gift of teaching hovering over you! If there is, changing diapers just won't do. Maybe you dread teaching Sunday school each week. Could it be that your gift is compassion, and you should be visiting nursing homes instead? You're missing the mark if you're a Sunday school teacher with no gift whatsoever of teaching while there are people who need you to use your gift of healing to touch them. You miss the mark trying to lead if you've been called to serve or give. You cannot just plug yourself into any ministry position and expect that you'll be fulfilled.

The Death Test

If you don't do the specific task that God has prepared and created you for, you potentially fall into what I call *dead works*, works that

147

aren't empowered by His Spirit. Many of us occasionally get caught up in a dead work. Do you want to know if you're guilty? Take the death test.

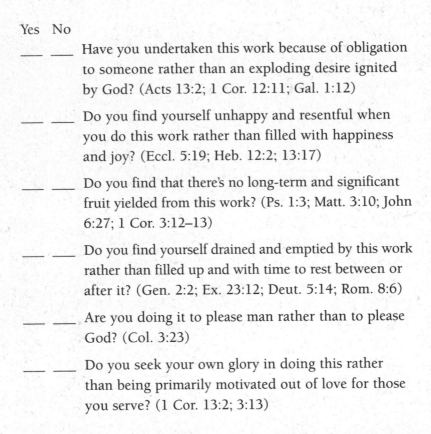

Yes No

___ ___ Have you undertaken this work because of obligation to someone rather than an exploding desire ignited by God? (Acts 13:2; 1 Cor. 12:11; Gal. 1:12)

___ ___ Do you find yourself unhappy and resentful when you do this work rather than filled with happiness and joy? (Eccl. 5:19; Heb. 12:2; 13:17)

___ ___ Do you find that there's no long-term and significant fruit yielded from this work? (Ps. 1:3; Matt. 3:10; John 6:27; 1 Cor. 3:12–13)

___ ___ Do you find yourself drained and emptied by this work rather than filled up and with time to rest between or after it? (Gen. 2:2; Ex. 23:12; Deut. 5:14; Rom. 8:6)

___ ___ Are you doing it to please man rather than to please God? (Col. 3:23)

___ ___ Do you seek your own glory in doing this rather than being primarily motivated out of love for those you serve? (1 Cor. 13:2; 3:13)

If you answered yes to most or all of the above, you're probably being distracted from your true calling by dead works. What a clever work of the devil. All the while, we actually think we're serving God, and we're more and more puzzled by the lack of results and fulfillment in our lives. Anytime we work outside of our gifting, we're likely to not accomplish much and to be left drained and depleted.

Are you discouraged and frustrated in your current attempt at ministry? Leave it for someone whose passion will be far more effective than your dread! Let's find out what you're really supposed to be doing.

Maybe you dread teaching Sunday school each week. Could it be that your gift is compassion, and you should be visiting nursing homes instead?

Gifted Works

The New Testament has five specific passages that, combined, list approximately twenty-three gifts appointed by the Holy Spirit. Most of us have gifts from this list; however, God can supernaturally gift *anything!* When God was building the Old Testament temple, He came down and offered a spiritual gift to a guy named Bezalel. After all, He needed someone to carve the ark of the covenant, to mold the lamp stand, and to set the stones. Check out Exodus 31:2–3: "See, I have chosen Bezalel . . . and *I have filled him* with the Spirit of God, *with skill, ability and knowledge in all kinds of crafts*" (italics added).

God's Spirit came into Bezalel and made him an intricate designer. Do you know what this knowledge did to my vision of the Old Testament artifacts? I used to think they must have been somewhat crude, but this verse changed my thinking. These had to be the most amazing works of art to hit the planet. God can fill you with amazing works, too, if you just dive into your spiritual gifts.

A Dialogue with God

I would like to encourage you to open up a dialogue with God about your supernatural gifting. I've found that His direction for me in this area comes over periods of years. For example, on May 24, 2002, when God first spoke to me about the spiritual gift of prophecy, it blew my mind! I was quite uncomfortable even with the term. But I wrote down what I sensed God saying and anticipated that He'd either say more to me in the future or I'd never have to deal with the word *prophecy* again. He said more! Between 2002 and 2005, the Lord prompted me to learn about this gift, and I recorded five significant revelations in my prayer journal.

The New Testament has five specific passages that, combined, list approximately twenty-three gifts appointed by the Holy Spirit. Most of us have gifts from this list; however, God can supernaturally gift *anything!*

My conversation with God continues as I discover multi-leveled layers to this gift and have had it directly confirmed three times through people who didn't know I was pondering it. Now, I don't consider myself to be a prophet with authority like Isaiah, and I don't have a position of prophecy as he did. I have a gift of forth-telling the Word of God, and it often presents itself through pictures in my head. I'm still figuring it all out.

Does this gift stretch your theological boundaries? Does the term *prophecy* mess with your previously conceived ideas of today's spiritual gifts? I understand. It messes with me too. But what good is a spiritual gift if it's a neat and tidy talent that just can be taught to us? It would limit it to a hobby . . . a human-size skill.

That would be completely contrary to God's teaching about spiritual gifts. They aren't meant to be completely understood or, perhaps, even all that comfortably received. Very often, women who are operating strongly in a spiritual gift tell me stories about how hard it was for them to accept the gift. Let's step forward to begin a dialogue with God to accept something God-size, shall we?

Your Spiritual Gifts

What are you spiritual gifts? Maybe you've known for a long time, or maybe you have no idea. The companion study guide for this book includes an inventory to discover yours. If you don't have the study guide, simply look at the gifts listed here and circle those that seem to be supernatural abilities about which God wants to open up a dialogue with you.

Begin a dialogue with God about your spiritual gifting. The entire body of Christ is depending on you to use it. It could have a globe-altering impact. It did when the parents of Samuel Kang prophesied over their young son. At a time when alien Shinto beliefs were still being forced upon Koreans, Mr. and Mrs. Kang chose to follow Christ, and they

Administration
You love to manage projects and/or big visions.

Exhortation
You write notes, give hugs, and love sharing advice.

Giving
You have resources of money and/or property that you find joy in sharing.

Evangelism
You find yourself talking about Jesus to perfect strangers.

Healing
You are impassioned to pray for the sick, and you've seen people healed through those prayers.

Ministry/Serving
You're the first to sign up to help wherever needed.

Mercy
You enjoy helping those who are hurting.

Wisdom
You are a great problem solver and truth teller.

Prophecy
When you pray, you feel God talking to you about circumstances and people. You always encourage the people involved.

Knowledge
You can explain God's Word in difficult situations.

Teaching
When you study the Word of God, you just have to tell others what you've learned!

Pastor/Shepherding
You enjoy helping others figure out how God wants them to live.

Faith
You are optimistic about God's hand in your life and lend others that faith in hard times.

told their young son, "You will become a pastor."[2] Young Samuel Kang did not like this prophetic word from his parents and rebelled against it.

Meanwhile, another with the gift of prophecy came to South Korea.

A man named Billy Graham.

In 1973, he stood in front of more than one million South Koreans with souls hungry for the gospel. It was the largest recorded Christian gathering up to that time and in a nation that had for so long shut Christ out.

Billy Graham didn't just share the gospel of Christ (forth-telling the Word of God), he predicted that Korea would become the base for preaching the gospel through Asia (foretelling the Word of God). Though the mass of people that stood before him could certainly go forth to share the Word, they were limited by South Korea's restrictions on foreign travel. They were just beginning to let God in. They weren't about to let Him get out.

More than thirty years later, it seems that both the Kangs' and Graham's prophetic words are true. In 1988, the South Korean government was forced to open the doors to foreign travel if they wanted to host the Olympics in Seoul. They did.

One of the missionaries eagerly praying and awaiting that was a very heart-changed pastor—Samuel Kang.

Today, South Korea sends more missionaries worldwide than any country but the U.S. And, if the U.S. interest in missions continues to drop as South Korea's climbs, it won't be long until the nation is number one. Leading the effort is the director of the Korean World Mission Association, Pastor Kang.

I'm not sure whose prophetic praying had more impact. The very public Billy Graham. Or the very unknown Mr. and Mrs. Kang. I know they both glorified God!

Making It Work

But to each one of us grace has been given as Christ apportioned it. This is why it says: "When he ascended on high, he led captives in his train and gave gifts to men."

—Ephesians 4:7–8

The second part of the adornment of charis is a specific, Spirit-given spiritual gift. I'd like you to meditate on the gift(s) God has pushed you to pursue. Specifically, I'd like you to ask Him what you are supposed to do with this gift. Where should you use it? How are you supposed to pursue understanding it?

15

Am I Enjoying God?

I knelt in the pew of the tiny little prayer chapel of the Billy Graham Evangelistic Center at Wheaton College. I pondered the great charge of two hundred girls waiting for me in the auditorium next door.

"Here we go again," I said to the Lord. "You'll do this, right?"

After dozens and dozens of speaking engagements to share God's heart, I still had to sequester my introverted self away for confidence before each event. I'd never have imagined this life God was orchestrating. Whatever happened to quiet Friday nights at home with a chick flick and a bubble bath? I was starting to spend most of mine with as many as a thousand teenagers wanting to seek God's heart through my teaching.

My mind raced back to a conversation I'd had with a good friend when my first book was released. "You'll have to speak now," he had said matter-of-factly.

"Not a chance," I said with certainty. I didn't much like speaking, and I loved being home.

"You believe in the message, right?" he'd inquired.

"Of course I do." I backtracked. "I also believe God will carry it."

He challenged me for just a few moments that day, but the bottom line was that he made me realize that I believed God could carry a message. I just didn't believe He could carry it through my voice. Writing seemed so much safer for this homebody.

It was not to be.

God would call me to speak. Again and again. Unbelievable.

"Lord, please do this once again," I whispered, begging again for the freedom to pursue His call. I stood to walk into the auditorium.

As I approached the front of the stage, I looked out at the teenage girls before me.

And then I felt it. That inexplicable feeling I got every single time I obeyed God with the spiritual gift of teaching to an audience. It felt like butterflies in my chest . . . right next to my heart.

And then I opened my mouth. I couldn't believe it, but I loved this. It was the greatest high I'd ever known.

To this day, my team has not solicited one single speaking event for me. And yet, the invitations come in. I still have to approach God's throne for passion to stand in front of an audience. I'm not afraid anymore. I just have a strong bent in me that wants to be alone rather than in front of people. (That's one way I know these gifts of teaching and prophecy are from God. They're not natural skills but ones God has gifted and developed.) I'm still every bit an introvert, but when I take the stage, the Holy Spirit takes over. And nothing in the world feels quite so wonderful. Please understand, I'm no Beth Moore. (Oh, to teach with such anointing!) But I've come a long way from my first public speaking experience.

My first speaking assignment was in college. My speech on table etiquette was supposed to be five minutes long. It was over twenty and filled with *um's* and *ah's*. My professor, Dr. Haffey, went in to her Advanced Public Speaking class that afternoon and announced that she'd "just heard the worst speech of her career." She went on to describe my speech. Too bad for her, I was dating a cute guy named Bob Gresh in that class, and he'd listened to me practice that speech the night before. Poor guy! Dr. Haffey was so embarrassed when Bob walked up after class and said, "That's my girlfriend who gave the worst speech ever!" (It was actually the beginning of a great friendship between the three of us.)

> This is how it feels to be in the dead center of the bull's-eye, to live in the heart of the mark. No matter what God calls you to, you'll find inexplicable joy.

My point? I'm not a natural speaker. God has spiritually gifted me with teaching and prophecy. When I speak, I feel God's pleasure. I am overcome with joy.

This is how it feels to be in the dead center of the bull's-eye, to live in the heart of the mark. No matter what God calls you to, you'll find inexplicable joy.

Mary Beth Chapman's Joy

Clinical depression.

That was the 1991 diagnosis for Mary Beth Chapman, wife of recording artist Steven Curtis Chapman. She says of that time:

> Will was a newborn, Caleb was one and Emily was finishing preschool. Steven was getting ready to embark on *The Great Adventure Tour* and we were also in the process of building a new home. In the middle of all that, I had to have emergency gall bladder surgery and Steven's parents divorced . . . I was physically and emotionally depleted and there were times I literally hid under the bed, I was so overwhelmed.[1]

Hiding under the bed? I've wanted to. Maybe you have too. But have you ever actually done it?

Mary Beth sought professional counsel and found that with medication, careful calendar planning, and counseling, she could live free of the great burden of depression. She simply had to keep things simple.

A simple schedule. A simple family. Everything was OK.

Then, a few years later, came a nudge from God: adopt a baby from China. (And little did she know, but she was also being nudged to start her own foundation to support the adoption of international children.)

I can only imagine the moments of fear and turmoil mixed with the excitement of following God's design for her life. Would this completely undermine the peace Mary Beth had found in balancing her life? Well, two adoptions (and one thriving foundation) later, Mary Beth said:

> It doesn't make any sense, but in the midst of all the craziness and sleep deprivation, I experienced—and still do—an underlying peace like never before. I can only attribute that to God. I think part of it is that until now, I haven't had such a sense of purpose and a knowledge that this is exactly where God wants me. That purpose—of daily meeting these precious little girls' needs and of helping to make it easier for others to adopt needy little ones overseas—gets me outside of myself and personal struggles.[2]

Mary Beth Chapman is glorifying God and *enjoying* Him. Have her circumstances changed? Yes, but not as she'd have planned on her own. She had to look with the eyes of her heart. It just didn't make sense in the physical realm. Her life did not become more quiet and more structured. It became the total opposite. She has now adopted three girls and started Shaohannah's Hope, a foundation to fund international adoptions. (I wonder what spiritual gifts she talked to God about? Hospitality, mercy, administration? Certainly she had to rely on His anointing for this big life change!) I'm quite certain her life has gotten louder and quite crazy.

But in it she has found joy.

Are You Enjoying God?

The writers of the Westminster Confession of Faith stated that there was one "chief end of man" and yet they included two very important things—to glorify God *and to enjoy Him.* The fourth question you must ask yourself in your quest to dive into the "heart of the mark" is one we've previously touched on. "Are you enjoying God?"

God sure wants you to. Hear Him speaking to you:

> *Delight yourself in the* LORD *and he will*
> *give you the desires of your heart.*
> —Psalm 37:4

> *You have made known to me the path of life; you will fill me with*
> *joy in your presence, with eternal pleasures at your right hand.*
> —Psalm 16:11

> *Rejoice and be happy in the* LORD.
> —Psalm 32:11 NCV

> *Without faith no one can please God. Anyone*
> *who comes to God must believe that he is real and*
> *that he rewards those who truly want to find him.*
> —Hebrews 11:6 NCV

159

The Heart of the Mark

God wants you to enjoy Him. The quest to glorify God and to enjoy Him is the biggest part of the mark. It's what I like to call the "heart of the mark." Without this in your life, you're missing the mark big-time. If you're following me, you understand that what I mean by that is this: failing to enjoy God is sin.

And while it's really a moot point to try to make this anything but a hedonistic quest, some certainly have made their service to God an obligation and their time with Him routine and unexciting. Perhaps you've found the part of your life you give to God in service unexciting. It may be because you've never taken time to dialogue with Him about your spiritual gifting, and you're stuck in dead works. Maybe it's because you have not yet dared to step out to walk in those spiritual gifts that test your faith because they press against your natural skills.

Adornment of Charis

Heart of the Mark

GOD'S BEST

the Ring of Grace

Have you struggled with spending time with God? Often these struggles come because we don't enjoy our time with Him. We squeeze fifteen minutes into our schedule and watch the clock to make sure we've reached the goal of how much time we will spend. If you're like me, you've had periods of time where you approach devotions with about the same enthusiasm as brushing your teeth or taking a shower. It's just what you do. Oh, God forgive us! Author John Piper says this in *Desiring God*: "If you come to God dutifully offering him the reward of your fellowship instead of thirsting after the reward of his fellowship, then you exalt yourself above God as his benefactor and belittle him as a needy beneficiary."[3]

We ought to come to God *expecting pleasure.* We should come to worship and to our quiet time not because we ought to but because we deeply desire and even crave the benefits of time with the God of the universe. In this selfishness alone is desire truly holy. C. S. Lewis says, "If we consider the unblushing promises of reward and the staggering nature of the rewards promised in the Gospels, it would seem that Our Lord finds our desires not too strong, but too weak . . . We are far too easily pleased."[4]

We are a self-satisfying people, but we don't come close to receiving the great rewards that we could. We settle for chocolate cake to fill a hunger that's not even physical, when we could be feasting on the all-satisfying food of the presence of God. We seek relationships to fill the craving of our insatiable desire for unfailing love, when only one love will never fail us. Truly, our desires are not too strong, but too weak.

The Joy of Chara

The Greek word for *joy* or *rejoice* is *chara.* Its meaning speaks of an exuberance or gladness of heart despite the physical realm. This is not happiness or peace. It's an underlying sense that all is calm in the depths though the surface doesn't appear to be safe at all.

I remember Corrie Ten Boom, a dear survivor of Auschwitz, talking about joy. Her sister, Betsie, was grateful to God when their barracks became infested with lice and fleas. Later they found out the infestation was what kept the Nazi guards from coming near the door. Corrie was free to read from her smuggled Bible and sing worship songs.

When I began to pursue God with all my heart and soul and strength, the circumstances of my life did not change right away. They couldn't. I had lessons to learn to equip me for my own path. But immediately, God began to impart joy—a certainty that all was calm, though the surface did not yet appear safe at all.

I remember a specific time when I knew that joy through reliance on God. There was no money in the accounts at our little marketing firm. None. Bob was out of town, leaving me in charge of our company. The mail wouldn't come until after the banks closed that day, and it was payday. Would I really have to call clients and make pleas to collect payments? Worse yet, would I have to tell our employees that we couldn't pay them today?

"Oh, God," I cried. "If there is any way You can send me money . . . I know we created this debt and don't deserve Your help, but we sure need it."

After a few moments of quiet, I blew my nose, wiped my raccoon eyes, and straightened my suit coat. I had a confident knowing that God was in control. Even if I did have to make phone calls and ask employees to wait for paychecks, I would do it in God's strength. I actually felt joy as I arrived back in the office to find a very happy bookkeeper.

"Dannah, you won't believe this," she said. "The mailman came three hours early today, and we got five huge checks. It'll more than cover payroll!"

Not the dramatic story of Mary Beth Chapman. My story is very ordinary. But even in the ordinary paying of bills, God brings His joy to the heart that seeks Him. Please notice that my joy came before God's provision was evident. It came because I spent time talking to Him about it. As I began to spend time with Him, His blessings began to bubble to the surface.

One day I simply could not go on a moment longer with the heaviness of the debt, the struggles in my marriage, juggling too many hours at work and not enough time with my kids, or the hopelessness of being stuck in it all. Tears rolled down my cheeks as I walked from one client's downtown building to my own office. "Please God, I need a friend so badly." I walked exactly half a block and, to my surprise, Debbie Cook, my pastor's wife, pulled her car over to the curb and stuck her head out of the car.

"Hey, get in." She smiled. I did. "I never come home this way," she bubbled. "I just took this turn a few blocks ago and there you were. I had to stop."

My despair turned to giggles as I shared with her how much I needed a friend.

My heart delighted in God. Though my life didn't change overnight, it was beginning to be filled with joy. God promises this to us when we pursue Him. The Psalmist writes: "You have made known to me the path of life; you will fill me with joy in your presence, with eternal pleasures at your right hand" (Ps. 16:11).

Even in the ordinary paying of bills, God brings His joy to the heart that seeks Him.

When you seek God with intensity, He'll show you your path, your own unique direction and purpose. *Only* on that path is chara found. You may still find challenges along the way, but each one will be met with this underlying joy as you bring them to God. Such passion is the only thing that will enable us to glorify God by reflecting His perfection, and only when we are that filled with joy for God will we be able to glorify Him by reflecting His moral excellence. John Piper says, "I know of no other way to triumph over sin long-term than to gain a distaste for it because of a superior satisfaction in God."[5]

The secret to hitting the heart of the mark is simply joy. If we do not find joy in our relationship with God, we will never glorify Him, and our boundary against sin will be weak and easily penetrated. Do you enjoy God?

His presence is the only place you'll find freedom. Second Corinthians 3:17 reads, "Where the Spirit of the Lord is, there is freedom."

Do you want freedom? Do you want to pursue God free from anything that restrains you in your choices or actions? Slow down, right now. Enjoy Him.

Making It Work

Where the Spirit of the Lord is, there is freedom.

—2 Corinthians 3:17

Are you enjoying God? If you're fully infused with His grace and pursuing your unique spiritual gifts in an environment that's right for your behavioral strengths, you'll be more likely to find joy. But ultimately, it is found in just being with Him.

When was the last time you spent one hour just being with Him? Want to rock your world? Schedule an hour to be alone with God today. You'll feel His presence. I promise. As you meditate on 2 Corinthians 3:17 and its truth revealed through the Samaritan woman's experience, ask yourself if you are enjoying God. Ask Him to show you what you need to do to find pleasure in Him.

Am I Glorious?

My mom handed me yet another Christmas gift.

I opened it.

"Mother Teresa!" I exclaimed as I pulled back the paper to find a beautiful book of photographs and quotes of her life work. I loved this woman I'd never met. The sensitivity with which she approached the poorest of the poor. The commitment to live in poverty as they suffered in poverty. The willingness to give up her own name to take on the simple name of a young nun who died of tuberculosis.

She took all of herself away, leaving only room for God to be seen.

Even when her own glory was pushed upon her with the coveted Nobel Peace Prize in 1979, she did not stand in it but stepped aside. There would be no fancy dinner to honor her. Instead, all the money would be used to feed the poor. There would be no speech of thanks, only a testimony of her Savior. Oh, to be like her!

I opened the book. The first page read, "Too many words . . . let them just see what we do. —Mother Teresa"

"Oh yes, Lord," I thought. "Let this be how I live."

And yet, I was very mindful as I prayed how real the temptation had become to stand in the glory rather than step aside to glorify Christ.

"Look at us!"

The apostles Peter and John were headed to the temple to pray. As they walked to the temple, they had to pass a gate called *Beautiful*. The ancient writer Josephus writes that it was wonderfully rich and ornate. Here at this gate, the crippled and poor often gathered, hoping to attract the kindness of the wealthy as there were no charities in that day.

As Peter and John passed by, a man crippled from birth attempted to capture their sympathy. He asked them for money.

The apostles, fresh with the power of the Holy Spirit, didn't take time to think of their plan. It is as if they both knew. The Scriptures read that they both spoke the same words. "Peter and John looked at him and said, 'Look at us!'"

Look at us! Look at us? Hold it. Shouldn't they have pointed this poor guy to God? Isn't that where he should be looking? Why didn't they say, "Look to God?" Why?

I believe it was because they were intimately aware that they were called to glorify Him—to reflect Him, to make Him known. They knew they were called to be glorious so that God would be recognizable to a man whose physical legs were crippled along with his spiritual eyes. He couldn't look with the eyes of his heart, so he had to look at them.

> They were called to glorify Him—to reflect Him, to make Him known. They knew they were called to be glorious so that God would be recognizable.

Peter and John were aware that they were about to give this man the gift of healing. (Can you imagine the butterflies in their beings at that moment?!) They were also aware that it was all they had to give.

"I don't have any silver or gold," says Peter. "But in the name of Jesus of Nazareth, stand up and walk!"

And he does. He jumps to his feet and begins rejoicing. And he glorifies God.

How? He runs through the streets, jumping and praising God. Ya know what I bet he was saying? "Look at me!"

When our lives are what God intended them to be, we can say, "Look at me," and the world will see Him.

Less Fame . . . More Glory

My husband has learned that in order for me to take even a remote interest in football, I need to know the players.

"Hey, that guy's wife is dying of the rare blue-footed-booby-bird syndrome," he'll shout as I walk by.

"Really?" I ask gullibly after seventeen years of marriage filled with practical jokes.

"Naw," he'll admit, "but . . ." and he'll go on to tell me something true and engaging.

Nothing has been more engaging than the truth of Kurt Warner, NFL quarterback and mighty man of God, who found himself in a cave a few years ago. My son grew up loving this guy, and in a minute you will too.

For years he prepared to be a professional football player only to find himself stacking groceries while working the night shift instead. It seemed he'd never rise up to be what his heart dreamed he could become.

Until . . . one day he got a shot. And that shot lead him to two Most Valuable Player awards and as many Super Bowl victories with him leading the way. He was applauded by the media and enjoyed becoming an author.

Oh, did I mention that he prayed a lot while stocking those shelves back at the grocery store?

On his First Things First Foundation Web site, Warner writes, "NFL experts have been trying to figure out the secret to my sudden success in the NFL. For me, it's easy and really has little to do with football. First things first—faith and family—that is my formula for success."[1]

My son has a few items signed by Warner, and not one is without a Bible verse. It was rumored that the only football card Warner would sign was the one he had printed himself, the one that explained on the back how the wide-eyed, proud recipient could have a relationship with Jesus, just like his.

Adornment of Charis

Heart of the Mark

GOD's BEST

the Ring of Grace

Now don't go weak at the knees if you're a single girl! Oh, OK . . . go a little weak. After all, isn't that the guy we all wished to marry when we were sixteen?

Well, don't be so quick. The highs never last too long. After a few years of fame, *Sports Illustrated* reported that "destiny decided to Ralph all over him."[2] Hand and shoulder injuries combined with a concussion took away Warner's finely tuned throwing skills. He fumbled six times in the season-opening game with the New York Giants that year. His coach took him out for the rest of the season and put him on second string. Until . . . quarterback Marc Bulger started having a tough time of it in a game against the Chicago Bears. When the coach saw Bulger losing it, he called for Warner to go in. This was it . . . Warner's moment for redemption, right?

Wrong.

Warner simply said, "Coach, to be honest, I don't think that would be the fairest thing to do to Marc. He deserves the chance to fight through it." So Bulger had his chance, leaving Warner to sit on the sidelines.

"I know I wouldn't have wanted to be pulled in that situation," Warner later said. "Besides, the Bible says do unto others as you'd have them do unto you. That's the example I'm trying to set."[3]

Now that's glorifying God. Warner had the chance to step back into the limelight. To pursue fame for himself. He didn't. He operated outside of his comfort zone when he affirmed Bulger rather than strapping on his helmet. Kurt Warner taught a very important lesson to boys like Robby Gresh and, maybe, your son. He taught them true character. He taught them good sportsmanship. And for those who are believers, he taught them to glorify God rather than to seek fame. He taught them something from the cave of his life that he couldn't teach them from the spotlight.

Am I contradicting what I said a few paragraphs ago? No, Warner was still saying, "Look at me!" He just wasn't saying it for the sake of his own fame. He was allowing his weaknesses to display Christ's strength in him.

The Heart of the Mark

Here in the heart, you'll ask yourself two questions for self-evaluation. The first is, "Am I enjoying God?" The second is, "Am I glorious?"

You and I are called to glorify God:

171

So whether you eat or drink or whatever you do,
do it all for the glory of God.
—1 Corinthians 10:31

We were chosen so that we would bring praise to God's glory.
—Ephesians 1:12 NCV

This is to my Father's glory, that you bear much fruit,
showing yourselves to be my disciples.
—John 15:8

Bring me all the people who are mine,
whom I made for my glory.
—Isaiah 43:7 NCV

Kurt Warner did. Peter and Paul did. God knows I'm giving it my best, but I have a long way to go. It's the core of what we're called to. The rest—whether we're pro football players or gifted healers, florists or moms, teachers or politicians—will come. We just need to be more consumed with His glory than our own fame.

There is no time in my life that I glorify God more than during private conversations. What I am in private with teenage girls that I minister to at my events is far more than I'll ever be in public. These are my greatest opportunities to glorify God by saying, "Look at me!" Look at my life and how God has made it whole.

Are you whole?

Are you free?

Are you glorifying God from the very center of your purpose?

The Rat Race

Sadly, the heart of the mark is where we start to get all messed up, which brings us back to where we began. We think glorifying God means we're supposed to jump into the rat race of Christian works, supposed to say yes to every request the church makes of us, supposed to be busy, busy, busy . . . but nothing could be a greater deception.

It's been a cold winter, and our garage is full of mice. I'm not happy about cleaning up after them. What is funny is that one night Lexi heard what she thought was her old hamster's wheel squeaking in the cage. She moved to the garage door and placed her ear up against the door. Convinced there was a mouse in the cage, she opened the door in a flash and flipped on the light. And there, in fact, was a tiny little mouse in her old hamster's cage.

We think glorifying God means we're supposed to jump into the rat race of Christian works ... but nothing could be a greater deception.

Now that little dude could have run from here to Florida if he wanted. (I'd sure like to do so about this time of year.) Instead, he finds a cage to run in.

How very much like that we are when we run back again and again to our dead works. Instead, God invites us to do God-size things in a God-size way in a God-size world. That doesn't *begin* with working. Though you will eventually step out of your cave or let go of your fish to move into Spirit-anointed, God-size works, it begins with resting in God. As the great Chinese evangelist Watchman Nee wrote:

Christianity does not begin with walking; it begins with sitting. Most Christians make the big mistake of trying to walk in order to be able to sit, but that is the reversal of the true order.

173

Christianity is a queer business! If at the outset we try to do anything, we get nothing; if we seek to attain something, we miss everything. For Christianity begins not with a big *do*, but with a big *done!*[4]

What we have all too often today is rat-race Christians doing, doing, doing and never sitting in the presence of God.

It's only when we're *with* Him intimately that we receive the power that gives us confidence to say, "Look at us!"

Mother Teresa's Secret

The great mother of Calcutta's poor was once asked about the secret to her worldwide success. After all, none of it was achieved by the spending of much money, and she started with only herself and masses of the poor. She never stopped caring for people one by one to devote herself to management or administration. She was called to tenderly love one person at a time. She was given great favor by world leaders even as she firmly but ever so softly used the public platform they'd given to her to renounce their own policies. (She once used an invitation from President Clinton to condemn his support of abortion.) Her ways were not of this world. How did she achieve so much with so little? "My secret is quite simple—I pray!" she told one man.

You should spend at least half an hour in the morning and an hour at night in prayer. You can pray while you work. Work doesn't stop prayer, and prayer doesn't stop work. It requires only that small raising of mind to Him. "I love you, God, I trust you, I believe in You, I need you now." Small things like that. They are wonderful prayers.[5]

In hiding away with God, Mother Teresa was quite visible to a world that needed to see Jesus. Her words and life did not cry for fame. They showed His glory.

Are you hidden away with God so that your life says, "Look at me"?

Making It Work

"Look at us!"
—Acts 3:4b

Did you spend an hour with God as I suggested in the last chapter? If not, let me reinvite you to give it a try. If you did, don't you want more of it? You can only say, "Look at me," with confidence if your life is hidden in the presence of God. Won't you step out of the rat race to sit with Him today?

PART FOUR

STEPPING INTO A GOD-DESIGNED LIFE

"The credit belongs to the man who is actually in the arena, whose face is marred by dust and sweat and blood; who strives valiantly; who errs, who comes short again and again, because there is no effort without error and shortcomings; but who does actually strive to do the deeds; who knows great enthusiasms, great devotions; . . . who at the best knows in the end the triumph of achievement; and who at worst, if he fails, at least fails while daring greatly, so that his place shall never be with those cold timid souls who neither know victory or defeat."

—Teddy Roosevelt

Daring Greatly to Step into the Ring

"Oh, God," I whispered as I settled into bed. "Help me teach these women what sin is."

I'd adjusted to a life of travel and teaching but found that to really be in the arena, God needed me working on lives I could rub up against. I found myself a bit disoriented as I entered once again into an unfamiliar place. Seven middle-aged moms had joined me for a Bible study, and the subject was sin. I'd spent much of the week studying, looking up Greek and Hebrew words, praying for a new way to approach it and a fresh desire to talk about it. I had done my homework. I just didn't have the plan yet. And the class was tomorrow morning.

"How do I show them what You really mean, God?" I asked and slowly began to drift off to sleep.

Then, I dreamed.

I saw a target with a thick neon ring around the bull's-eye. The middle was filled with a huge heart, and in between was a flurry of activity and design.

I would wake up the next morning with a fresh and vivid memory of the picture in my head.

And I understood completely what I was to teach.

"No one will want to read that book," said a kind advisor when I explained that exploring the biblical language of sin seemed to uncover an exciting map that helps us find our God-designed life.

"It'll never happen." That was the first response I got when I first dared to approach an editor about this book. That was six years ago. It took a lot of time, but God's perfect time has finally unfolded for me to write this book. I hope you can see how tender it is of God to give us the concept of sin. It can be a compass to our purpose. Living in the bulls-eye of God's appointment for our lives is the key to freedom from sin. Well, you've just about finished reading it. How've we done together? I think it's been a pretty exciting journey. And yet, the journey is just beginning.

It's time for you to dive into the ring of grace, live out the adornment of charis, and experience the heart of the mark. These are the three parts of God's bulls-eye. They help you to define God's design for your life. It's time to start living free from the restraints in choices and actions that fears and sins put into your life.

It's time to be, as the Word of God describes it, blameless.

Adornment of Charis

Heart of the Mark

GOD'S BEST

the Ring of Grace

Be Blameless

Ephesians 1:4 sums things up so beautifully for us, but we must look at it carefully. It says, "He [God] . . . chose [you] *before the creation of the world . . .* to be holy" (italics added). God chose you! When? Before the creation of the world. Just imagine that before He created this world, He knew what you were designed to accomplish in it. He's chosen you to be holy, and the next phrase says you're to be blameless. And it *does* mean sinless—free from anything that restrains you in your choices or actions to pursue God. What a high calling!

God has called you to be a perfect reflection of Himself. Will you or I ever truly be sinless? My theology doesn't take me there. So what is God calling us to? Well, the word *blameless* comes from the Greek words *AA* (alfah), which connotes the beginning, and *meros*, which means *to remember*. To remember what? I think it's calling us to remember how vibrant and fabulous our life was meant to be when God planned it before the creation of the world. Before sin marred our beings. That's a long time back to remember. But what's there is fantastic. This is a call to remember what we were created for in the beginning.

Oh, that our spirits would remember the life God designed for us!

> God chose you! . . . Just imagine that before He created this world, He knew what you were designed to accomplish in it.

The bottom line is that you were brought into this world literally birthmarked for greatness. God put this invisible bull's-eye in the deepest place of your being. It's etched there as an invitation to live within the ring—the dead center. It won't go away. It's meant to be there, and you can live with it as if it's an unsightly smudge, or you can let it be your compass to the life God designed for you.

I know what I'm choosing. How about you?

Daring to Step In

Do you dare to step into the bull's-eye of God's purpose for your life? I invite you.

You've got the tools.

Now, step in.

Take the rest of this chapter to write the next step. Just start journaling as you meditate on Ephesians 1:4, 13b–14. Let God show you what your next step is going to be. How will you enter into the ring of grace to live free from restraint in pursuing God?

When you've finished, come back for one more dose of encouragement. You'll want it along the way, I promise!

Making It Work

In Christ, he chose us before the world was made so that we would be his holy people—people without blame before him . . . God put his special mark of ownership on you by giving you the Holy Spirit that he had promised. That Holy Spirit is the guarantee that we will receive what God promised for his people until God gives full freedom to those who are his—to bring praise to God's glory.

—Ephesians 1:4, 13b–14 NCV

Using these thoughts from God, make a journal entry here. Set some goals based on what He tells you from these Scriptures combined with what you've learned in this book.

18

Daring Greatly to Stay in the Ring

Well, here I sit.

It's 1:34 in the afternoon, and I'm leaving for Africa in less than twenty-four hours. (Remember the peanut butter?) As I walked out of my office earlier this morning, I matter-of-factly said, "I need to go finish my book."

Dree, my friend and booking manager, burst into hysterics. (You have to know her.) Then she said with an exaggerated yawn as she made fun of me, "Ah, yeah, I'm gonna just go finish a book, and then in a few hours I'm going to fly halfway around the world to build a figgery."

We both laughed at her mistake. I hope we build a piggery and not a figgery. It would be bad if my poor volunteers anxiously awaited the arrival of pigs to put into our freshly constructed pig-pens, but instead someone showed up with a bunch of figs. Don't you agree?

Well, this is my wonderful place of purpose. I love it here. The air is fresh, and my heart is free.

How about you? You know, if you've done the work of this book, you now have a step-by-step plan to enter into the ring of grace.

What will you do with it?

> Then birds of prey came down on the
> carcasses, but Abram drove them away.
>
> —Genesis 15:11

There is just one more powerful word of truth you need to meditate upon before you begin to live out your plan. It comes to us from Genesis 15. I've told you about the fish and the caves. I haven't warned you about the birds. They are real stinkers!

Birds of Prey

In Genesis 15, we find Abraham (who is still Abram) making perhaps the most holy sacrifice of the Old Testament. It is the sacrifice that would seal in blood the covenant between God and the people of Israel. This is *the* Old Testament covenant. A holy moment, to be sure. You'd think there might be an angelic sighting or at least a little stillness in the air. Nope. Instead, Abram finds himself in a frustrating situation. His sacrifice is being eyed by birds of prey.

Now, I was walking Stormie, my wonder dog, through a nearby field the other day, and she rustled up some birds. Just little mourning doves, as far as I could tell, but what a show they put on. They took noisily to flight, clearly disrupted by her presence. They circled and circled her, and then they would land. They'd let her get just close enough to pounce, and then they'd take to the air again and tease. It was such a sight that I wondered, what *did* Abram go through with these birds of prey that God actually took time to record it?

Birds of prey are nasty creatures. Those who have analyzed their feeding rituals refer to it as repulsive. Perhaps this is what led Ancient Egyptians to believe that birds of prey ate the livers out of dead people. They don't do that, but their beaks are perfectly crafted to pick bits of meat from bones. Bits of meat. They don't get a whole meal in one bite. They come back again and again and again. In this process they often "vocalize." Lots of birds have melodious vocalizations. Not birds of prey. They make short, shrill, often eerie sounds, and some even hiss. Abram had his hands full. At a most holy moment, he was running around waving his arms like a maniac.

What a picture.

Why did God take time to record it?

Could it be that when we rise up to pursue God, free of restraints, the birds of prey will swoop down upon us to devour our sacrifice? Oh, how many times I've experienced this. Again and again and again, when I step out to pursue God, free from restraint, Satan sends in his birds of prey.

> When we rise up to pursue God, free of restraints, the birds of prey will swoop down upon us to devour our sacrifice.

Drive Them Away

Knowing that they're coming is half the battle. I mean, it'd be great if I could just tell you life will be peachy now that you're living in the life God designed for you, but it won't be. Most certainly, you'll be bothered by birds of prey.

What do you do? God victoriously records for our encouragement what He saw from heaven: "But Abram drove them away!"

Drive them away. How? Well, we've come full circle, haven't we? Go back to the beginning of this book. It was all about filling you with truth to overcome your fears. The birds of prey almost always come in the form of our fears.

You do have the hope to drive them away.

You do have the ability to be satisfied while you drive them away.

You do have the time to slow down and drive them away.

Your past does not disqualify you; it equips you to drive them away.

You will not fail. You will drive them away. And just like Abram, that tenacity will allow you to walk into the very center of the life God designed for you. What adventures you'll find there when you overcome these fears.

Well, I'm off to withdraw thousands of dollars from the bank. Apparently, there aren't a lot of ATMs where I'm going. It's time to dive into yet another plan that God has for my life.

You know, the "figgery."

What's your next adventure?

Acknowledgments

Thanks!

Other than *And the Bride Wore White*, no other book has simmered so long in my soul. This one gestated longer than an elephant! (Nothing female should have to be pregnant for twenty-two months. I cannot wait to ask God what He was thinking when He did that to our poor pachyderm friends.) I first received the concept for this book in the year 2000 when I was just beginning to live in the life God designed for me. I'm so grateful that after seven years, the time and team were right to bring it to you.

I'm first very grateful to the Thomas Nelson team, which was led by Brian Hampton during this book's release. Brian is an incredible man of his word. He was faithful to this book during a chaotic time. *And* he knows how to say my name for which I'm most grateful! It's *Dannah* not *Dana*. (Not that there's anything wrong with Dana. It's just not my name.) Paula Major was the team member who rivaled Brian for his faithfulness. She is patient and calm in the face of multiple deadlines swirling around her desk. Thanks, too, to Bryan Norman, Brandi Lewis, Greg Steilstra, Stephanie Newton, Belinda Bass and, not least of all, Joey Paul!

My Pure Freedom team runs my world for me so that I can write. Thanks, Eileen King, Jen Wilton, and Gary Arblaster for keeping things rolling during this season. Thanks to my designers, Julia Ryan (for the book cover) and Andy Mylin (for the internal graphics).

Thanks to my wonderful family. Bob, I promise you that I am more in love with you than ever. I'm so glad that you are in the life God designed for me. It wouldn't be as wonderful without you. I love you. Robby and Lexi, you are the best kids a mother could ask for. You are patient, adaptable, supportive, and always ready with a good laugh when the deadlines get to me. And Mom and Dad, thanks for setting the stage for me to have the best possible chance of having a great life. I truly do have one!

Mostly, thank you to my great God and King for designing a fulfilling and amazing life for me. I am in awe of all that you have entrusted to me.

What adventure is next?

Notes

Chapter 1
Are You Free to Live the Life God Designed for You?

1. The Barna Group, "Most People Seek Control, Adventure and Peace in Their Lives," www.barna.org/FlexPage.aspx?Page=BarnaUpdate&BarnaUpdateID=68, 1 August 2000.
2. Rick Warren, *The Purpose Driven Life* (Grand Rapids, MI: Zondervan, 2002), 31.

Chapter 2
Fear #1: There's No Hope for Me

1. http://news.bbc.co.uk/1/hi/world/americas/1561791.stm, 31 May 2006.
2. Donna VanLiere, "Love Endures," *LifeLines* (Fall 2004), 4–6.

Chapter 3
Fear #2: Nothing Will Ever Satisfy Me

1. This paragraph was inspired by John Piper, *Desiring God* (Sisters, OR: Multnomah, 2003), 91. I discovered John Piper's book during the time that I was learning to truly enjoy my time with God. Much of this chapter is inspired by his diligent work in *Desiring God.* I've learned to live it!

Chapter 4
Fear #3: There's No Time to Fix It

1. Brent Curtis and John Eldredge, *The Sacred Romance* (Nashville, TN.: Thomas Nelson, 1997), 165.

Chapter 5
Fear #4: My Past Disqualifies Me

1. Mike Rimmer, "Divorce, Healing and the Old, Old Hymns," www.crossrhythms.co.uk/articles/music/Divorce_Healing_and_the_Old_Old_Hymns/7983/p1, 1 Sept. 2002.
2. Ibid.
3. Ibid.
4. Scott Hahn, *The Lamb's Supper* (New York: Doubleday, 1999), 105.
5. Henry Blackaby and Claude V. King, *Experiencing God: Knowing and Doing the Will of God* (Nashville: Lifeway, 1994), 99.

Chapter 6
Fear #5: I'm Going to Fail

1. Brennan Manning, *The Signature of Jesus* (Sisters, OR: Multnomah, 1996), 29.
2. "Is Addiction Just a Matter of Choice?" http://abcnews.go.com/US/print?id=90688, 26 May 2006.

Chapter 7
God's Battle Plan for Freedom

1. Many of the observations about Lewis and Freud were taken from Armand M. Nicoli Jr., *The Question of God: C. S. Lewis and Sigmund Freud Debate God, Love, Sex and The Meaning of Life* (New York: Free Press, 2002). I'm an avid Lewis reader and am strongly sensitive to the disconnect between Freud's life and chosen profession—that of helping people to experience mental and emotional health. This book delighted my heart as it brought much of my philosophy about Freud to life and caused him to "meet" my beloved author!
2. Quoted in Nicoli, *The Question of God*, 158.
3. Ibid.
4. The Barna Group, "Views on Quality of Life Are Most Influenced by Money and Faith,"www.barna.org/FlexPage.aspx?Page=BarnaUpdate&BarnaUpdateID=137, 24 April 2003.
5. Anne Ortlund, *The Gentle Ways of the Beautiful Woman* (New York: Inspirational Press, 1998), 50.
6. The Barna Group, Ibid.
7. Philip Yancey, *Rumors of Another World* (Grand Rapids, MI: Zondervan, 2003), 144.

Chapter 9
Letting Go of Your Fish

1. Corrie Cutrer, "No Place Like Home," *Today's Christian Woman*, November/December 2004, 57.
2. Ibid.
3. Ibid., 58.

Chapter 10
Snares Are Not Set in Caves

1. Gene Edwards, *A Tale of Three Kings* (Wheaton, IL: Tyndale, 1992), 29–30.

Chapter 11
Being Still in Your Cave

1. Gene Edwards, *The Prisoner in the Third Cell* (Wheaton, IL: Tyndale, 1991), vi.

Chapter 12
Do I Need a Fresh Infusion of Grace?

1. Hahn, *The Lamb's Supper*, 22.

Chapter 13
Am I Working in Agreement with My Created Personality?

1. Charles F. Boyd, *Different Children, Different Needs* (Sisters, OR: Multnomah, 1994), 27.
2. Dr. William Moulton Marston was a noted psychologist of his time and wrote

The Emotions of Normal People in 1928. In it, he unveiled his personality profiling system. The system, most commonly used as the DiSC test, is used freely in many different forms, some more accurate than others. I like it because it enables you to get a grasp of how you best operate and what might frustrate you, but you don't have to have training to measure yourself. Incidentally, Dr. Marston also introduced the comic world to Wonder Woman. What a life!

3. John and Cindy Trent and Gary and Norma Smalley, *The Treasure Tree* (Nashville:Tommy Nelson, 1992). John Trent and Gary Smalley initially wrote about the four personality types in a chapter in their book on relationships, entitled *The Two Sides of Love* (Colorado Springs: Focus on the Family Publishing, 1999).

Chapter 14
What Is My Supernatural Abilitiy?

1. Barna Research Online, "Awareness of Spiritual Gifts Is Changing," www.barna.org/FlexPage.aspx?Page=BarnaUpdate&BarnaUpdateID=81, 5 Feb. 2001.
2. Rob Moll, "Missions Incredible," *Christianity Today*, March 2006, 28.

Chapter 15
Am I Enjoying God?

1. Camerin Courtney, "Surprised by Joy," *Christianity Today*, November/December 2003, 44.
2. Ibid., 43.
3. John Piper, *Desiring God* (Sisters, OR: Multnomah), 97.
4. C. S. Lewis, "The Weight of Glory," *The Weight of Glory and Other Addresses* (New York: Macmillan, 1962), 3–4.
5. Piper, *Desiring God*, 11.

Chapter 16
Am I Glorious?

1. www.kurtwarner.org/aboutus.html.
2. Rick Reilly, "Ram Shackled," *Sports Illustrated*, December 8, 2003.
3. Ibid.
4. Watchman Nee, *Sit, Walk, Stand!* (Wheaton, Ill.: Tyndale, 1977), 14.
5. Michael Callopy, photographer, *Works of Love Are Works of Peace* (San Francisco: Ignatius Press, 1996), 103.

Weekend Getaway with The Author!

Dear New Friend:

I really want this book to work in your life. Two things make that happen: accountability and encouragement. For that reason, I'd really love to see you enjoy this book with a group of friends who can hold you accountable. (There's nothing like a good friend to whack you over the head now and then!) Sometimes we just have a hard time being objective about where we are and where we really need to be. A group of friends can help you with that.

I'd like to be one of those friends.

Please join me for the *Five Little Questions* Weekend Getaway at St. Joseph's Institute, a spiritual retreat center and spa that's been applauded by the likes of the *Washington Post*. I'll facilitate the weekend, offering key teaching points as you develop your life action plan. You'll also enjoy dynamic group conversation and beautiful moments of solitude. (And, of course, you can opt to add a few spa services to your weekend!)

❝You can find out when our next Five Little Questions weekend is by visiting my website at www.purefreedom.org.❞

" can't wait to help you discover the life that God
" r you.

GO DEEPER

WITH DANNAH'S FIVE LITTLE QUESTIONS:
the Guided Journaling Experience

"If you slow down and answer these five questions thoroughly, you'll have an action plan to live in the fulfilling and adventuresome life that God designed for you."

—*Dannah Gresh, Five Little Questions*

Five Little Questions That Reveal the Life God Designed for You is a quick overview filled with inspiration to live a more fulfilling and adventuresome life. But sometimes it takes more than inspiration; you have to roll up your sleeves and do some work. Dannah Gresh wants to be your personal life coach.

In *Five Little Questions: The Guided Journaling Experience*, Dannah provides specific questions, quizzes that help you answer those questions, diagrams, and deeper scriptural insight to treasure as you seek the life God designed for you. The study guide includes:

- Twelve weeks of personal Bible study
- A step-by-step Life M.A.P. (My Action Plan)
- A spiritual gifts inventory
- Marston's personality inventory
- A deeper look at biblical proofs for the Five Little Questions
- Thought-provoking questions for personal journaling
- A leader's guide for group study

To purchase *Five Little Questions: The Guided Journaling Experience*, visit your favorite Christian bookstore or Dannah's Web site at www.purefreedom.org.